The papers in this volume first appeared in Opening The Bible: Selected Writings of Antony Campbell SJ, ATF Press, 2014. All reprinted with permission.

InterfaceTheology:
Volume 4, Number 1&2, 2018

Editor Board
Revd Dr John Capper, University of Divinity, Melbourne
Dr Philip Kariatlis, St Andrews Greek Orthodox Theological College, Sydney

Editorial Manager
Mr Hilary Regan, Publisher, ATF Theology, PO Box 504 Hindmarsh. SA 5007, Australia. Fax +61 8 82235643.

International Reference Group
Rev Dr Vicky Balabanksi, Uniting College for Leadership and Theology, Adelaide
Rev Dr Ted Peters, Pacific Lutheran Theological School, Berkley
Rev Dr Murray Rae, University of Otago, Dunedin

Subscription rates
Print: Local: Individual Aus $55, Institutions Aus $65.
Overseas: Individuals US $60, Institutions US $65.

Interface Theology is a biannual refereed journal of theology published in print, epub and open access by ATF Press in Australia.
The journal is a scholarly ecumenical and interdisciplinary publication, aiming to serve the church and its mission, promoting a broad based interpretation of Christian theology within a trinitarian context, encouraging dialogue between Christianity and other faiths, and exploring the interface between faith and culture. It is published in English for an international audience.

ISSN 2203-465X
Cover design by Astrid Sengkey. Text Minion Pro Size 11

ISBN: 978-1-925679-36-6   soft
         978-1-925679-37-3   hard
         978-1-925679-38-0   epub
         978-1-925679-39-7   pdf

An imprint of ATF Theology part of the ATF Press Publishing Group.
ATF (Australia) Ltd.
PO Box 504
Hindmarsh SA 5007
Australia
www.atfpress.com
Making a lasting impact

A Kaleidoscope of Biblical Articles

Antony Campbell SJ

Table of Contents

Dei Verbum:
Literary Forms and Vatican II—
an Old Testament Perspective

(Original: God's Word and the Church's Council)

The invitation offered by the fiftieth anniversary of a Council document is a marvellous opportunity to look at the nature of an ecumenical council (such as Vatican II) and the nature of its documents. The
nature of neither can be taken for granted. In days gone by, Council
documents culminated in a series of propositions, each ending with
'anathema sit',—let any person holding this view be considered anathema, an outsider. Vatican II did not do this. At the earlier Councils, it
was probably felt that the anathema would hold its force for all time.
The passage of time would make clear that with the changing circumstances of Church and culture that was not the case. 'Anathema sit'
might be best understood as 'we're really serious about this.' It is the
responsibility of historians to determine how long that seriousness
lasted. It is also the responsibility of historians to determine whether
Council documents were a base from which the future might be
developed or a culminating crown summing up the preceding developments or a stopgap while a process of theological reflection continued. Which was *Dei Verbum* and how does it look fifty years later?

John O'Malley is emphatic that the literary form of the documents
from Vatican II is radically different from what preceded it, going back
to the beginning with the Council of Nicaea.[1] Most of the documents
of Vatican II sought to address the world; those of its predecessors
addressed the Church. The code for the former would be 'pastoral';
for the latter, 'legislative and judicial'. The two must therefore be used
quite differently. As a rule, in the 'legislative and judicial', the Council

---

1. John O'Malley, *What Happened at Vatican II* (Cambridge, MA: Harvard
University Press), 11 and *passim*.

laid down the law for what was to be believed and condemned the errors opposed to that belief. The 'pastoral' quality of the Vatican II documents means that quite opposed positions can be found within the same document because quite opposed positions could be found within the same Church.

Dei Verbum provides as good an example of this as any. Early in the piece (1962), dissatisfaction with the initial schema for discussion was registered at sixty percent. In 1965, after four years of stubborn resistance from a group favouring tradition over scripture as the primary vehicle of revelation, the final vote was almost unanimous, 2344 in favour and six against. One side was not massively outvoted; the stubborn minority had not seen the light and caved in under pressure; instead, the text was such that both sides could vote for it. As one participant put it: 'We must not simply substitute the declaration of a different school of thought, but rather produce something acceptable to all'.[2] Congar clearly understood 'that Paul VI wanted to secure a large consensus of the Fathers and that that presupposed compromise'.[3] These Vatican II documents must be read very differently from their predecessors.

It is standard practice for Latin documents emerging from the Vatican to be known by their opening words. In this case, *Dei Verbum* (Word of God) can be misleading. The document is a Dogmatic Constitution on Divine Revelation, as it is correctly entitled. It is not exclusively concerned with the inspired word of scripture, as the title *Dei Verbum* might suggest. Its concern goes beyond the biblical word to touch on the many ways in which God is revealed to God's creatures, some dealt with in detail and some in a passing reference.

Close inspection makes clear that *Dei Verbum* intends to affirm an overall image of the past and encourage a sure march into the future. In its own words: 'Following in the footsteps of the councils of Trent and of First Vatican, this present Council wishes to set forth the authentic teaching about divine revelation and about how it is handed on' (*DV*, #1).[4] The document *Dei Filius* from Vatican I leaves

---

2. Dom Basil Butler, President of the English Benedictine Congregation, in Yves Congar, *My Journal of the Council* (Adelaide, SA: ATF Theology, 2012), 198.
3. Congar, *Journal*, xxii.
4. Translation throughout from Walter Abbott (editor), *The Documents of Vatican II: All Sixteen Official Texts Promulgated by the Ecumenical Council, 1963–1965, Translated from the Latin* (London: Chapman, 1966).

open the possibility of access to God by reason. Vatican II affirms it bluntly: 'God . . . can be known with certainty from created reality, by the light of human reason' (*DV*, #6). On the complex question of scripture and tradition, Trent's 'scripture and tradition' [et] is dealt with far more extensively by Vatican II (*DV*, ##7–10].

It is desirable that space should be given to the issue of scripture and tradition. It was a major sticking point at the time of the Reformation; Luther's 'sola Scriptura' [scripture alone] was a rallying cry of significance. A proposal at Vatican I affirmed that revealed truth was to be found *partly* in scripture and *partly* in tradition (*partim . . . partim*). The Council rejected this formulation, because the evidence for it was not there; instead it adopted the alternative more flexible, formulation 'scripture and tradition' [et].[5] I have seen a 'penny catechism' from the archdiocese of Sydney in the 1930s, that asked the question whether all revelation was to be found in scripture. In flat contradiction to Trent, it replied: certainly not; divine revelation was to be found partly in scripture and partly in tradition. Within the Roman Catholic Church of those days, Sydney was probably not alone in knowing what to do when it was a question of denying Protestantism or adhering to Trent. Let the Protestants lose.

That Trent's idea was right is clear; that its formulation was unsatisfactory is evident. Given the importance of the matter, it is small wonder that Vatican II devoted considerable effort on the issue. Anyone with ecclesial experience of ecumenism will be well aware that the Roman Catholic Church's approach to issues of divine revelation will often be different from that of other Churches. That difference can be summed up globally by the term 'tradition'. Exegetes (aka. biblical interpreters) may struggle with words, sentences, or passages; Churches more often grapple with matters of greater weight. Of course, tradition plays a role, along with scripture, in keeping faith alive and well—and moving in the right direction.

At this point it is time for a moment to take a look at the reality of an ecumenical council. It is not a wondrous gathering of mystical truth-sayers who have the insight and intelligence to guide the Roman Catholic Church securely for the next century or two. It is a cross-section of the present-day Roman Catholic Church, with its

---

5. Council of Trent, Decree concerning sacred books and traditions to be received; Denzinger-Schönmetzer. #1501).

conservative factions and its liberal factions, with its wise folk and its weirdos. The leadership will be tugged forward and backward. The future of the Church will be reflected in that tugging.

When a couple of thousand bishops, archbishops, and cardinals meet in a single place (St Peter's) for a relatively short period of time (four sessions) for a major ecumenical Council, it is a moment of massive significance for the whole of Western Christendom. The participants in such a gathering will reflect a wide range of people—as for believers, so for bishops—from astute front ends of thoroughbreds at one extreme of the range to the rear ends of hard-working draught horses at the other. An ecumenical council is not a gathering of learned theologians; it is not a gathering of naïve believers; it is not a gathering of specialist guides to lead the faithful toward the future. Far from it. A council is a mirror of the Church it represents. Its role is to reflect on where that Church is now and where it might best be going in living to the full the good news of Jesus Christ, of God's love for us in the ordinariness of our lives. It is a gathering of a couple of thousand leaders, reflecting a billion or so believers, including the learned and the naïve, the high-power administrators and the pastorally committed, the elite and the common-or-garden, the wise and the stupid. It is precisely the wide-ranging complexity of this variety that makes this gathering of such massive significance.

Vatican II was summoned by the much-loved Pope John XXIII. The word primarily associated with both Pope and Council was *aggiornamento*. Modernisation, up-dating, bringing up to date are all accurate enough as translations go but a bit facile. It is not easy to catch the force of the image. It is not a matter of throwing open the doors and windows and letting daylight into the structure. The force of the image is day rather than light. Left untouched by the word is whether doors and windows are thrown open to invite 'day' into the structure or to invite the contents and people within the structure to move out into the 'day'. When revelation is under scrutiny, the issue then is whether the forces of day are to enter the structure and further burnish the understanding of revelation or whether the occupants of the structure are freed to move out into the day and inspect the revelation that is being understood out there. This may be very abstract imagistic language. What it points to is highly significant. Where is revelation to be sought? Inside the bureaucracy of the Church or outside the bureaucracy among the believing faithful? The answer 'both' is easy; articulating what this answer means is not easy at all. It is this 'aggiornamento', this openness of the church to its surrounds, that is probably the high point and lasting contribution of Vatican II.

The dogmatic constitution on divine revelation, *Dei Verbum*, as its readers will gratefully acknowledge, casts its net wide, embracing whatever is of value to those who believe. So, for example, the document speaks early on of God buoying us up with the hope of salvation, with 'His promise of redemption' and it quotes Genesis 3:15 (*DV*, #3). A little later on, it insists that attention must be paid, among other things, to *literary genres* (*DV*, #12). In the reference to Genesis 3:15 as a promise of redemption and in the reference to the importance of literary genres for understanding the meaning of a text, *Dei Verbum* invokes two widely different approaches to the understanding of biblical text, approaches as different as the front and rear ends of a thoroughbred. For the historical-critical exegete, Genesis 3:15 has as its purpose 'to describe the phenomenon that enmity exists not merely in a determined situation but has grown to a continual state, something like an institution'.[6] Tradition, on the other hand, reaches back to Irenaeus (second century) for an understanding of the passage as a prophecy about Christ (seed of Mary) and the devil (seed of the serpent). Says Westermann, a relatively conservative modern exegete, 'there are two main reasons that do not allow such an interpretation'[7]—which we will pass over here.

Irenaeus was the second bishop of Lyons, in France, and was a major figure in the writings of the early Church; he lived a couple of hundred yards down the road from where, for four years, I lived and studied theology. It is said that Irenaeus first moved the interpretation of Genesis 3:15 from Eve's descendants and snakes to Jesus and Satan. This is a perfect example of what, since the term was coined in 1925, has been called *sensus plenior*. In the *New Jerome Biblical Commentary* (*NJBC*, #71.50) the *sensus plenior* is described as 'the deeper meaning intended by God but not clearly intended by the human author, that is seen to exist in the words of Scripture when they are studied in the light of further revelation or of development in the understanding of revelation.' Its discussion peaked in the work of

---

6. Claus Westermann, *Genesis 1–11* (Minneapolis, MN: Augsburg, 1984); German original, 1974, 259.
7. Westermann, *Genesis 1–11*, 260.

Fr Raymond Brown, SS;[8] interestingly, there has been almost no discussion of *sensus plenior* since 1970. Further comment in the *NJBC*, almost certainly from Ray Brown, goes on to say: 'the fact that advocacy of the SPlen [that is, *sensus plenior*] had its roots in distrust of excesses in patristic typology and allegory gave SPlen exegesis a more cerebral and cautionary aura. Reasonable homogeneity with the literal sense was insisted on, and the SPlen was seldom invoked even by strong supporters.' Two points can be underlined: (i) the *sensus plenior* was distinguished from the literal sense; (ii) reasonable homogeneity with the literal sense was insisted on.

There is a notion that recurs almost as a mantra in various formulations in a hugely important book on the Eucharist, *In Breaking of Bread*: 'The heritage of our belief is unsatisfactory, but that does not stop it from being revered.'[9] That applies precisely to what *Dei Verbum* has done in this case: it combines an unsatisfactory interpretation of Genesis 3:15 that is part of a past to be revered with an insistence a little later on the importance of attention to *literary genres*.[10]

This not an isolated example. The document, *Dei Verbum*, quietly insists on the reverence owed to tradition and equally quietly insists on the openness to the future owed to biblical studies.

The Council has done what it had to do and what has such massive significance. It has dressed the vine in such a way as to yield maximum fruit to the members of its Church, both learned exegetes and generalist believers. There are some, for example, who find the bridal language of late Isaiah ('with everlasting love I will have compassion on you,' Isa 54:8) a superb base for prayer; there are others for whom other passages echo spousal abuse ('double for all her sins,' Isa 40:2) and cause revulsion more than anything else. Both sorts of passages are in canonical scripture; both sorts of passages have meaning in the right moments. Ecumenical councils must be careful not to exclude what may have meaning in the various right moments of our lives, whether in scripture, in theology, or in faith.

---

8. Raymond Brown, *The Sensus Plenior of Sacred Scripture*. STD Dissertation. (Baltimore, MD: St Mary's University, 1955).

9. PJ FitzPatrick (a Catholic priest, in the department of philosophy at the University of Durham), *In Breaking Of Bread: The Eucharist and Ritual* (Cambridge: Cambridge University Press, 1993), 322.

10. Or 'literary forms'; original Latin, 'genera litteraria'.

The full text of *Dei Verbum* on literary genres reads: 'In determining the intention of the sacred writers, attention must be paid, among other things, to *literary genres*.' With ancient texts, authors can only be reached through the text. So the phrase 'the intention of the sacred writers' is a convenient shorthand for the exact meaning of the text around the time of its composition. Scholars need to know this; often believers need not. There is often no one single reading of the text that alone is right and proper. There is the text to be read by scholars, the text to be read by preachers, the text to be read for prayer and reflection—and so many more. The danger of cross-pollination is real but avoidable. The beauty of a conciliar document is its ability to leave room for many such readings.

Form criticism, the primary discipline relating to the literary genres, was and is a scholarly means of getting at the appropriate academic meaning of a text. It asks the question that must be asked: what sort of a text is this? All too often that question has been answered glibly and wrongly: this text is history or this text is divine communication. In all cases, this text is to be proclaimed as the word of God. But as Msgr Raymond Collins has put it in the *NJBC*, 'This traditional formula, apparently simple, is extremely complex and polyvalent'.[11]

The polyvalence is evident. There are many words attested in Scripture that provoke reflection on the 'traditional formula' word of God. For example: there is the psalmist at prayer, marvelling at God's concern for us (Ps 8); there is David mourning for his Jonathan (2 Sam 1:25–26); there is a psalmist venting his rage most horribly (Ps 137:8–9); there is God's word, from a prophet wrapped in mystery, 'just as the LORD loves the people of Israel, though they turn to other gods' (Hos 3:1); there is God's contradictory word, powered by identical motivation (the evil inclination of the human heart) brought together by the mythmaker, 'I will blot out from the earth the human beings I have created . . . nor will I ever again destroy every living creature as I have done.' (Gen 6:7; 8:21); there is God's word that must witness to a theologian at work, 'Let us make humankind in our image, according to our likeness' (Gen 1:26). 'Complex and polyvalent' is putting it mildly.

---

11. Raymond Collins, 'Inspiration', 1023–33 (article #65) in *The New Jerome Biblical Commentary (NJBC)* edited by RE Brown, JA Fitzmyer, RE Murphy (Englewood Cliffs, NJ: Prentice Hall, 1990), #65:67.

However there is more complexity and more polyvalence to deal with. Sayings such as 'thus says the LORD, "the word of the LORD" saying of the LORD' are common in the prophetic books, as might be expected. But there are also three prophetic stories (1 Kgs 13; 22; and Jer 28) that suggest the presence of thought in this area then and the need for it now. One prophet lies to another in the name of the LORD; acceptance of the lie brings the other prophet to his death (1 Kgs 13). In the divine council, one of the host of heaven proposes to be a lying spirit in the mouths of the royal prophets and God approves; it leads to the divinely willed death of Israel's king (1 Kgs 22). The conclusion of the scene is the statement: 'So you see, the LORD has put a lying spirit in the mouth of all these your prophets; the LORD has decreed disaster for you' (1 Kgs 22:23). Finally, at the start of a carefully structured story, the prophet Hananiah, in all the solemnity of the temple in the presence of priests and people, proclaims: 'Thus says the LORD of hosts, the God of Israel: I have broken the yoke of the king of Babylon' (Jer 28:2). At the end of the story, Jeremiah is given the last word: 'And the prophet Jeremiah said to the prophet Hananiah, 'Listen, Hananiah, the LORD has not sent you, and you made the people trust in a lie. Therefore, thus says the LORD: . . . Within this year you will be dead . . .' In that same year, in the seventh month, Hananiah died' (Jer 28:15–17).

The chilling conclusion is formulated by Robert Carroll: 'when the divine word may be a lie, prophecy itself becomes an activity in which true and false are indistinguishable.'[12] Carroll's concluding quote from ER Dodds (in the context of the Pythian oracle) may stifle criticism of Hananiah, but it does little to reassure: 'Anyone familiar with the history of modern spiritualism will realise what an amazing amount of virtual cheating can be done in perfectly good faith by convinced believers.'[13] Clearly, in the world of ancient Israel the complexity and polyvalence of the word of God was troublesome.

For *Dei Verbum*, the phrase 'word of God' cannot be applied exclusively to the sacred scriptures; on occasion, it is given a wider meaning. 'Sacred tradition and sacred Scripture form one sacred deposit of the word of God, which is committed to the Church' (*DV*, #10). While such a statement may betray the origins of the document, it needs to be taken into account for understanding the final form. Reflection on

---

12. Robert Carroll, *Jeremiah*, OTL (London: SCM, 1986), 548
13. *Jeremiah*, 550.

the books of the Old Testament emphasises the *imperfect* and the *provisional*. 'These books, though they also contain some things which are incomplete and temporary, nevertheless show us true divine pedagogy' (*DV*, #15).

In all this, it is probably not unfair to smell some confusion. A wise course is to allow the future to sort out that confusion. That is precisely what *Dei Verbum* does when it turns to literary forms. But first, as noted earlier, an element bearing on that wisdom is worth noting. The commission responsible for *Dei Verbum* had been given a preliminary draft prepared by the Theological Commission, with a first chapter, 'Two Sources of Revelation' (that is, scripture and tradition). In due course, a vote was taken whether the draft should be returned for rewriting. Sixty percent voted to return it, falling short of the two-thirds majority required for this step. John XXIII pulled papal rank, sided with the sixty percent majority, and constituted a new joint commission to recast the text.[14] This accounts for the place of scripture and tradition early in the document, more in line with Trent's final text than the more polemical and inaccurate 'partly . . . partly' of an earlier version at Trent. Rather more important, this early vote in 1962 pointed to the need for delicacy on the part of the commission's authors who could only count on about sixty percent of the votes of their commission. Bold innovation was not to be the order of the day. The success of the approach adopted is indicated by the final vote of the full Council: 2334 for and six against.

The language of the document is: 'Those who search out the intention of the sacred writers must, among other things, have regard for *"literary forms"* . . . The interpreter must investigate what meaning the sacred writer intended to express and actually expressed in particular circumstances as he used contemporary literary forms in accordance with the situation of his own time and culture' (*DV*, #12).

There is a phrase here that is a quiet reminder that any Council document is a creature of its time and that also serves to banish any whiff of infallibility that might be about. The phrase, 'the intention of the sacred writers', was a helpful shorthand for invoking the historical–critical method and turning one's back on some of the fallacies of centuries past—which of course is precisely what *Dei Verbum* is

---

14. Roderick MacKenzie, 'Introduction' to *Dei Verbum*. Pages 107–10 in *The Documents of Vatican II*, edited by Walter Abbott (London: Chapman, 1966).

doing. By now, any interpreter of text should know that the intention of a writer is mediated by the meaning of the writer's text. There is no other way of reaching an ancient writer's intention. What should be said is not 'the intention of the writer' but 'the meaning of the text'. A quibble of this kind is critical for interpreters of text; it is of no concern to ordinary people and of no concern to bishops, archbishops, and cardinals. The presence of the phrase is a valuable reminder that the document is a creature of its time.

Dei Verbum is emphatic on the role of the exegete: 'It is the task of exegetes to work according to these rules towards a better understanding and explanation of the meaning of sacred Scripture so that through preparatory study the judgment of the Church may mature' (*DV*, #12). Naturally enough for a council document, this task is performed within the church: 'All of what has been said about the way of interpreting Scripture is subject finally to the judgment of the church' (*DV*, #12). The portrayal of this may be more easily said—'it is clear, therefore, that sacred tradition, sacred Scripture and the teaching authority of the Church, in accord with God's most wise design, are so linked and joined together that one cannot stand without the others' (*DV*, #10)—than made tangible in the flow of church life.

There is an adage that applies in many professions: it is not so much what is said but what is not said that can be so very revealing. That is certainly the case with *Dei Verbum*. The insistence on the necessary place of literary forms in interpretation is not hedged around with prohibitions or cautions. The reality of literary forms is to be embraced by those searching out the meaning of God's communication. Naturally, since the communication is with the church, in order that 'the judgment of the Church may mature' (*DV*, #12), the church's oversight is present.

The choice of 'literary forms' as the shorthand for modern biblical studies is peculiarly apt. At the core of these literary forms is the discipline of form criticism. It came on the scene at the beginning of the twentieth century, with a view to supplementing source criticism (German: *Literarkritik*), which was considered by scholars such as Hermann Gunkel and Hugo Greßmann to have completed a necessary job.[15] About the time of *Dei Verbum*, form criticism was at its peak; that peak has passed and form criticism today is waning. It was

---

15. For details, see Antony Campbell, 'The Emergence of the Form-critical and Traditio-historical Approaches', chapter 31 in volume III/2 of Magne Saebø (editor) *Hebrew Bible / Old Testament: The History of Its Interpretation* (Göttingen: Vandenhoeck & Ruprecht, forthcoming).

hoped that scientifically describable literary forms could be identified and associated with specific settings (*Sitz im Leben*). That hope has been disappointed and replaced by an enhanced trust in intuition, validated by careful study. The question, however, has been raised and will not go away: what sort of a text is this? No longer can it be automatically assumed that texts are either history or divine communication. *Dei Verbum*'s picture of the 'principal purpose to which the plan of the Old Covenant was directed' (*DV*, #15) may be challenging; the identification of smaller units may be more troubling yet. The question, 'what sort of a text is this?', must be asked, even if answering it is troublesome. The necessary follow-up to this question cannot be avoided; it must be answered. This follow-up question is: why has this text, in this form, been preserved in sacred scripture? One answer is the invitation to go think, the invitation to reflection on the matters involved, an invitation that can be offered by both creator and creature and that can be relevant down the ages. Other answers may be revealed as the future unfolds.

Dei Verbum has the comment that these books [Old Testament] 'contain some things which are incomplete and temporary' (*DV*, #15). The New Testament reflects the reality of a God who has embraced the weakness and fallibility of human life, 'true God and true man', in no way 'exempt and cut off from the divinely given but flawed world in which we live and die'.[16] Because we do not escape the vulnerability and incompleteness of the world in which we find ourselves and which we have been given, not escaped in the person of Jesus Christ, not escaped either in the words of sacred scripture, how then are troubling passages in scripture to be dealt with? The Talmud, the authoritative body of Jewish tradition, comments on two passages in Deuteronomy that are rightly troublesome. Regarding the first (Deut 13), 'The destruction of a whole community because of idolatry (verses 13 ff) never occurred nor will it ever occur. The sole purpose of the warning is that it might be studied and that one might receive reward for such study';[17] regarding the second, according to which the wayward or defiant son will be stoned to death (Deut 21:18–21), commenting on a tradition that says this law was never operative, the Talmud records the following: 'If so, why was it written in the Torah?

---

16. FitzPatrick, *Breaking of Bread*, 341.
17. Tosefta San 14:1.

To study (more) and to obtain reward therefrom' .[18] Study, presumably, reached the conclusion that such a law was inappropriate, that such a view could not be held. We might reach similar conclusions. In relation to following another god (Deut 13:3), the use of common sense is commended: 'Is it really possible to "follow" God, who is described (Deut 9:3) as a "devouring fire"? Rather, you should follow His attributes: as He clothes the naked, so must you; as He visits the sick, comforts the mourners, and buries the dead, so must you.'[19]

Early on, I borrowed the terms 'complexity and polyvalence' from Msgr Collins; with them we are not at a great distance from the term 'mystery'. The final chapter of *Dei Verbum* takes us in this direction. The chapter opens with the affirmation that 'The Church has always venerated the divine Scriptures just as she venerates the body of the Lord, since from the table of both the word of God and of the body of Christ she unceasingly receives and offers to the faithful the bread of life, especially in the sacred liturgy' (DV, #21).

We might do well to see an invitation here to place our understanding of the role of God in the ownership of the scriptures in much the same category as our understanding of the eucharist. Over two or three thousand years, believers have associated the Bible with God in an intimate and sacred way. Various believing bodies and various believers have articulated this association between God and Bible in various ways. What may best embrace this variety is the concept of mystery.

I have borrowed earlier from PJ FitzPatrick the notion that 'the heritage of our belief is unsatisfactory, but that does not stop it from being revered'.[20] This is said after careful study of medieval language around transubstantiation and equally careful study of recent attempts to replace it (courtesy of phenomenology). A summary of FitzPatrick's work may be drawn from his own words: 'What matters in eucharistic belief is what has always mattered, namely that the reality of what we receive is the Risen Lord; and what matters in the belief is not constricted by the categories of obsolete modes of thought, and not compromised by the incapacity of language to seize it.'[21]

---

18. San 71a.
19. Sotah 14a. The material above has been taken from Gunther Plaut, *The Torah: A Modern Commentary* (New York: Union of American Hebrew Congregations, 1981).
20. *Breaking of Bread*, 322.
21. *Breaking of Bread*, 309.

To paraphrase for sacred scripture: 'What matters in belief regarding God's role in sacred scripture is what has always mattered, namely that the reality of what we have in scripture has God in some way ultimately responsible for it; and what matters in the belief is not constricted by the categories of obsolete modes of thought as to how that is to be understood, and God's role is not compromised by the incapacity of language to seize it.'

Dei Verbum, the document that began with Trent and the traditions that preceded it, that looked to the future with unfettered endorsement of literary forms, and that ended with the word of God and the body of Christ in the eucharist, is a document that has surely done well. Familiarity with the Council leaves no doubt that the battle raged on many fronts between the Curia and the Ecclesia, with the latter victorious while on the scene. The words of Paul VI at the United Nations, 'Jamais plus la guerre' ('no more war') can be taken to heart. The Curia should never again be at war with the Ecclesia. It may take a century or two to work out the balance, but the balance between centre and periphery is essential to the leadership of the Church.

Past History and Present Text: The Clash of Classical and Post-Critical Approaches to Biblical Text

(original: ABR 39, 1991)

This paper is concerned with the current clash of academic approaches to the biblical text, specifically that of the Older Testament. These clashing approaches could be designated critical and literary, or classical and post-modern, but perhaps classical and post-critical catches the issue best. The new concerns—once structuralist, then canonical, now predominantly literary—are with the present text. Both enchantment and disenchantment seem to have had their role to play.

Enchantment with the biblical text as literary text is as old as the Bible's origins. The endeavour to bring this enchantment to fruition in compelling interpretation has, over recent decades, been fraught with difficulties. There is a new and welcome move afoot with more determinedly professional literary scholarship being brought to bear upon biblical interpretation. This move is still in its infancy. In a number of published examples it is problematic; the theoretical coherence with critical study is far from fully worked out. In this paper, I will be sticking to my last and offering the contribution of a reflective practitioner, which I believe I am, rather than that of a literary theoretician, which I am not. Theory has to keep in touch with the realities of the biblical text. It is these realities I seek to explore here.

Disenchantment has played its role in the recent emergence of a series of new approaches to the biblical text. Perhaps the compounding increase in the complexity of knowledge and skills demanded of the scholarly exegete has effectively stolen the Bible from its ordinary readers. Certainly, the inadequacy of the exclusively critical approach has made itself felt. It is forcefully expressed by a colleague in ascetical/mystical theology:

> It is now clear to everybody that the historical-critical
> approach, however valuable, is woefully insufficient. It alone
> will not put us in touch with the underlying mystery; it alone
> will not bring us to those eternal realities towards which
> the Scriptures point; it alone will not enrich our lives with
> mysticism.[1]

The key here is the phrase, 'it alone'. The historical-critical approach is valuable and often indispensable; but it is not the be-all and end-all of exegesis or biblical study. The question remains: once critical study has robbed us of our first innocence, is there a literary innocence which may be legitimately regained?

Naturally, individual studies vary. Among the examples of recent approaches there is reason to question whether in their essential functioning some have returned to a pre-critical position, or whether we are witnessing a further development in the sequence of critical disciplines (that is, text, source, form, tradition, and redaction criticism), or whether again some are signalling a genuinely post-critical phase in the study of the biblical text. Significant shifts have occurred. The cultural mindset which dominated the disciplines of biblical interpretation had its roots in the early nineteenth century and in developments in the classical and historical disciplines. Literary approaches to the task of biblical interpretation, with their roots in the late twentieth century, are having a significant impact on this formerly dominant cultural mindset. Some shifts can be sketched, without attempting to be exhaustive.

Significants Shifts

1. Shift in attitude towards the aim of interpretation

Once upon a time, it was said that the aim of critical interpretation was 'to determine what the writer intended to say and the first readers could and must have understood'.[2] Nowadays, I would prefer to say

---

1. William Johnston, *The Wounded Stag* (London: Fount Paperbacks, 1985), 25.
2. Quoted from Kümmel with regard to Schleiermacher by Edgar Krentz, *The Historical-Critical Method*, Guides to Biblical Scholarship (Philadelphia: Fortress, 1975), 24.

that it is to determine the meaning of the text—in other words, what the text says.[3]

Ideological issues aside, experience has taught that this change of language brings with it a change of mental focus. 'Intention of the author' is open to the intentional fallacy, to be corrected by attention to the text. 'Intention of the text', the terminology of the FOTL project, is still an invitation to personify the text, again to be corrected by attention to the text itself.[4] Language which focuses initially and primarily on the text forces a more direct attention to the source of meaning in the phenomena of the text.[5] This is not to deny or decry the place of the author, but to insist on the focus of our attention. With Paul Ricoeur, I cannot conceive of a text without an author, but the author is known only through the text and our attention must therefore be directed to the text without distraction.[6]

2. Shift in attitude toward the aim of historical-critical scholarship
Once upon a time, the aim of historical-critical scholarship was the recovery of history: the history of Israel itself, the history of Israelite literature, the history of Israel's literary forms, the history of Israel's

---

3. Should this sound too bland, it may be balanced by the insight given paradoxical formulation by Paul Beauchamp: 'Expliquer un text est, a toujours été, dire ce qu'il ne dit pas'—to exegete a text is, and has always been, to say what it does not say! (*Création et séparation: étude exégétique du chapitre premier de la Genèse* [Bibliothèque de Sciences religieuses; np (Aubier Montaigne/ Editions du Cerf/ Delachaux & Niestlé/Desclée De Brouwer, 1969], 15). Failure to see the paradox is not license for criticism or parody.
4. FOTL: the series, The Forms of the Old Testament Literature, published by Eerdmans, Grand Rapids.
5. I gratefully acknowledge that my conversion to this language is due to the sustained efforts of Stephen Prickett.
6. 'L'intention de l'auteur n'est pas son vécu psychologique, son expérience, ni l'expérience de la communauté à jamais insaisissable car déjà structurée par son discours. L'auteur est précisément celui que dénonce ou annonce le texte, par rétro-référence à celui qui l'a écrit . . . pour ma part, je ne concevrais pas ce que pourrait être un texte sans auteur, un texte qui n'aurait été écrit par personne . . . ce qu'il importe de découvrir, c'est que la notion d'auteur n'est pas une notion psychologique, mais précisément une grandeur herméneutique, une fonction du texte lui-même' (P Ricoeur, 'Esquisse de Conclusion', in R Barthes, *et al, Exégèse et herméneutique* [Paris: Editions du Seuil, 1971), 292–93. See also my *The Ark Narrative (1 Sam 4–6; 2 Sam 6): A Form-critical and Traditio-Historical Study*, SLBDS 16 (Missoula: Scholars Press, 1975), 195–97

theology. Nowadays, while all these are important, the primary aim should be moving toward interpreting the text with historical consciousness and critical awareness. 'Historical-critical' refers less to the goal of study and more to the attitudes of the practitioner. A baneful over-emphasis on history is tending to yield place to an appropriate concern for faith and theology or other issues.

A substantial contributory factor to this shift is the recognition that many of our scriptural texts are themselves concerned primarily not with the facts but with the meaning and the proclamation that can be woven from them. Redaction criticism points to this for the gospels. In the Older Testament, the duality of evidently contrasting accounts for both creation and flood, for exodus from Egypt and entry into Canaan, for the occupation of the land and the emergence of statehood—to mention only these—point in the same direction. They point to the narrative biblical texts as texts of faith, written from a stance of faith with a view to promoting faith.[7]

3. Shift in attitude toward the interpreter
Once upon a time, the emphasis was on the ideal of 'impartial and objective research'.[8] Nowadays, we are likely to prefer language about informed and responsible research as the ideal. Many factors have given subjectivity a better press than was formerly the case.

4. Shift in attitude toward the redactor
Once upon a time, the redactor was an ever-available and definitive explanation for any perceived clumsiness or incoherence in the text. Nowadays, redactors are coming to be recognised as consummately careful people and compilers or preservers with authorial status.[9]

---

7. See AF Campbell, 'Old Testament Narrative as Theology', in *Pacifica* 4 (1991): 165–80.
8. See Krentz, again with regard to Schleiermacher (*Historical-Critical Method*, 24).
9. See Shemaryahu Talmon's description of the Tannaitic fifth-century scribe: 'a man of many parts, a comprehensive literate who could be author, editor, transmitter, scribe or copyist when performing different aspects of his profession' ('The Textual Study of the Bible—A New Outlook', in *Qumran and the History of the Biblical Text*, edited by FM Cross and S Talmon [Cambridge: Harvard University Press, 1975], 336; see also 381). In this context, we may note Robert Polzin's comment—rightly inveighing against the tendency to brush redactors aside as clumsy and therefore a self-sufficient explanation for incoherence in the text: 'Is the narrative hand "crude"—what critics usually mean when they write *redactional*—or "careful"—what I mean when I write *authorial*?' (*Samuel and the Deuteronomist* [San Francisco: Harper & Row, 1989], 57). The phenomenon he pillories is only slowly fading from the exegetical scene.

5. *Shift in attitude toward the text*

Once upon a time, it might have been taken for granted that a composite text was not available as a whole for interpretation, since it was no more than the sum of its sources. Nowadays, with the change in attitude toward compilers and redactors, there is a demand for the final text to be interpreted in its own right.

Alongside these aspects, there is the question of the root cause for the resistance by much of traditional scholarship to approaches based primarily on the present text. If it is more than mere curmudgeonly dislike for change, it is important to know what is at stake. One area in particular is significant here: the question whether compilation and redaction allow the present text to be claimed as a text in all cases and invariably.[10]

We are so accustomed to the world of the printed book and the computerised recovery of information, it is immensely difficult to conceptualise a world in which books were written but not printed. In such circumstances, what use were written texts put to and what was their audience? How much was for private reading and how much for public? Did written texts accurately reflect their oral performance, or were oral performances based on texts, yet developing and expanding far beyond them? Without files or footnotes, how were valuable items to be preserved, which might not fit particularly well with a given text? Or how were dissenting views recorded and recovered? On all this vast area of the storage, recovery, and disseminating of information in ancient Israel we know very little. Yet it is significant for understanding the texts and the purposes they served.

6. *When the text is not always a text*

A useful working definition of a text is given by Harald Weinrich: 'A text is a meaningful (that is, coherent and consistent) sequence of

---

10. Polzin expresses this trenchantly in a criticism of the present writer. 'As I suggested in the Introduction, a relevant matter in this regard may be a scholar's view of the final text: does it appear so incoherent, ideologically speaking (because of the complicated process that the scholar believes lies behind its historical composition and because of the supposed crudity of its redactors), that any full-blown account of it as "narrative functioning as a vehicle for theology" ... would be an unsatisfying and embarrassing exercise?' (*Samuel and the Deuteronomist*, fn 15, 237). In the particular instance, Polzin unjustifiably overlooks the limits imposed by the length of a journal article; the wider application of the comment is nevertheless valid.

language signs between two evident breaks in communication.[11] The correlation with Zellig Harris's definition of an utterance is worth noting: 'any stretch of talk, by one person, before and after which there is silence on the part of that person.'[12] The increasing number of literary studies which assume or argue for the literary unity of the biblical text raises the issue of whether the biblical text is, in fact, always a text.[13]

We often use the term 'biblical text' to designate a sequence of words on a manuscript or page. When we pay attention to an understanding of 'a text' such as Weinrich's—a meaningful (that is, coherent and consistent) sequence of language signs between two evident breaks in communication—we have to ask whether discussion of the 'present text' may often involve a confusion of the two senses of text and whether this has serious consequences.

The question becomes acute when we take note of an observation associated by Weinrich with his definition of text. He remarks: 'Even arbitrarily juxtaposed pieces constitute in this sense evident (quasi-metalinguistic) breaks in communication.'[14] Is it possible that on occasion the juxtaposition of material by redactors or transmitters constitutes such a break in the sequence of communication that we are no longer correct in referring to the juxtaposed pieces as a text (in the strict sense)? If such a possibility exists, must we conclude that an indispensable step in all interpretation is to ascertain the existence and limits of the text as a text, technically understood, which is to be interpreted?

---

11. 'Ein Text is eine sinnvolle (d.h. kohärente und konsistente) Abfolge sprachlicher Zeichen zwischen zwei auffälligen Kommunikationsunterbrechungen' (Harald Weinrich, *Tempus: Besprochene und erzählte Welt*, third edition (Stuttgart: Kohlhammer, 1977); first edition 1964, 11.

12. ZS Harris, quoted in John Lyons, *Introduction to Theoretical Linguistics* (Cambridge: Cambridge University Press, 1968), 172.

13. In normal usage, phrases such as 'the text', 'the biblical text', 'the present text' certainly denote words on a page and also automatically include the notion of a text in the strict sense. In this paper, I shall retain this common usage. 'A text', with the indefinite article, is adequate in most circumstances to denote a text in the strict sense of the term; the qualification can be added explicitly when needed. In these terms, the issue under consideration is whether it is justifiable to assume automatically that 'the biblical text' is always 'a text' in the strict sense.

14. 'Auch willkürlich angelegte Schnitte schaffen in diesem Sinne (quasi-metasprachliche) auffällige Kommunikationsunterbrechungen' (Weinrich, *Tempus*, 11).

A critical element in this regard is the explication given by Weinrich for the qualification 'meaningful': that is, coherent and consistent. Coherence and consistency are relative terms. In using them, we claim a 'competence' to determine what is coherent or consistent in a given piece of literature or in the literature of a given culture.[15] If we were totally out of touch with the canons and conventions of ancient Israelite literature, we would not be able to understand the Hebrew scriptures. But insofar as we do not have any explicit and exhaustive description of these canons and conventions, we need always to proceed with caution, basing assertions on careful analysis of comparable passages.

In my observation of the Bible, I believe we encounter texts which may be better understood and given meaning better by interpretations which do not assume their unity, the assumption that they constitute a text. Certain aspects of this phenomenon need exploration and clarification. The issue might be said to be basically which of the three 'C's' is dominant in any given text: communication, conservation, and contradiction or modification (change).

- Communication, plain and simple, usually leads to a unified text.
- Conservation may interrupt such a text to point to another and different text or tradition. I think, for example, of the tree of life in Genesis 2–3 or the special collection of Davidic traditions in 2 Samuel 21–24.
- Contradiction or modification may seek to express a viewpoint which is diametrically opposed to that of the coherent literary

15. A brief treatment of the issues is given by John Barton, *Reading the Old Testament: Method in Biblical Study* (London: Darton Longman and Todd, 1984), 11–16. A good example of what is meant is provided by a note of Polzin's: 'Fokkelman's remarks on the apparent incoherence between and within chapters 16 and 17 [of 1 Samuel] are, in my opinion, unsatisfactory because they assert that *in this particular case* the Bible's "consistency requirements" are different from ours (*Narrative Art*, volume 2, 144ff.). There is no doubt that in many respects ancient and modern consistency requirements are different; the question here, however, is whether the type of "inconsistency" represented, say, by the known–to–Saul David of chapters 16:14–23 and 17:32–39 and the supposedly not–known–to–Saul David of 17:55–58 is an example of one of these differences. I maintain that such a supposed inconsistency as this would have been as obviously unacceptable to an ancient Israelite as it is to us' (*Samuel and the Deuteronomist*, fn 19, 258–59). The only source for Polzin's conviction is his experience of the consistency requirements of the Bible in other texts.

text, and may do so at the cost of substantial incoherence without sufficient integration to form a literary text.[16]

So a methodological step must be the inquiry whether a text is straightforward communication, or contains a dominant element of conservation, or is strongly marked by the expression of contradiction or modification. In the latter cases, the question has to be carefully investigated whether the text can be understood in such a way as to constitute a text in the strict sense.[17]

At this point, it is appropriate to move to three texts which can function as useful exemplars of the three different possibilities of communication, conservation, and contradiction or modification. In the first, in my judgement, a unified text has been created through composition (communication); in the second, two versions of a story have been preserved in combination, without achieving a unified text (conservation); in the third, different opinions have been given expression in a careful composition (contradiction/modification).

1 Samuel 1–7

A debate has existed, at least since Wellhausen in 1878, over the relationship of chapters 1–3 and chapters 4–6 in 1 Samuel. More recently, in a difference of opinion between myself and PD Miller and JJM Roberts, it has focused on whether a substantial part of 1 Samuel 2 belonged to the Ark Narrative or not.[18] Put in this way, the question is argued as one of authorial identity. I believe, however, that it is fundamentally a present-text question.

There is neither space nor reason for going over the arguments in detail here; they are all available.[19] The issue is a theologically signifi-

---

16. Over and above these, of course, there is M Noth's concept of the 'enrichment' of texts in the Pentateuch or elsewhere. Also significant is my concept of the reported story (see 'The Reported Story: Midway between Oral Performance and Literary Art', in *Semeia,* 46 [1989]: 77–85).

17. This is the aspect which is so frequently omitted, as Polzin, for example, rightly complains.

18. Campbell, against the inclusion, *The Ark Narrative,* above, note 5; Miller and Roberts, for the inclusion, *The Hand of the Lord: A Reassessment of the 'Ark Narrative' of 1 Samuel* (Baltimore: Johns Hopkins University Press, 1977).

19. See my discussion in 'Yahweh and the Ark: A Case Study in Narrative', in *JBL,* 98 (1979): 31–43.

cant one. Does Israel's narrative present its God as one who punishes the nation as a whole for the cultic and sexual sins of two priests and the alleged failure of their aged father to discipline them effectively? Or is there no causal connection between the loss of the ark and the sins of the Shiloh priests, so that the causes need to be looked for elsewhere?

For Miller and Roberts, for example, it is the former. The early part of the narrative (1 Sam 2:12–17, 22–25, 27–36) 'both describes the sin and announces the consequent punishment. This part of the narrative provides the motivation for all that follows. It gives an explanation for what would otherwise be an utterly inexplicable event—the defeat of Israel and the seeming defeat of Yahweh at Ebenezer'.[20]

My primary argument is that the text in 1 Samuel 2 does not sustain this interpretation. The narrative looks forward to a time of dishonour for the family of Eli, when they are replaced by another priestly family in the service of the king, a punishment normally understood to reflect Solomon's banishment of Abiathar in favour of the family of Zadok.[21] Specifically, the death of Eli's sons, Hophni and Phinehas, on the same day is to be a sign for Eli of this punishment. A sign is not to be confused with what it signifies.[22]

In my view, unless one takes for granted that chronological sequence is to be equated with causal sequence, a careful reading of the text of chapter 2 indicates that it is not predicting chapter 4 as the punishment of the Elide sins, and a careful reading of chapter 4 shows no sign of any attempt to explain the at–first–sight inexplicable defeats by reference to these sins and their punishment.

This is not a matter of genetic pre-texting, with an exclusive interest in sources and no interest in the present text. It is a question of giving serious attention to the meaning of the present text. In a critical reading of the text, it is possible to account for this lack of causal

---

20. Miller and Roberts, *Hand of the Lord*, 61–62.
21. See M Tsevat, 'Studies in the Book of Samuel', in *HUCA*, 32 (1961): 191–216.
22. The key text is: 'See, a time is coming when I will cut off your strength and the strength of your ancestor's family, so that no one in your family will live to old age. Then in distress you will look with greedy eye on all the prosperity that shall be bestowed upon Israel; and no one in your family shall ever live to old age' (1 Sam 2:31–32). This is more than the loss of two sons in a single day. There is no suggestion that the loss of the ark precipitated a period of prosperity in Israel; the reference is surely to the monarchy.

sequence by seeing the text as a composition of separate traditions. In a post-critical reading of the text, it is possible to be aware of this difference in origin and still interpret the movement of the text as a whole.[23]

While Wellhausen's comment that it is beyond doubt that chapters 1–3 were written with chapter 4 in mind would need a lot of nuancing today, it does acknowledge the presence of links between the texts and the direction of those links.[24] I have no difficulty in accepting that 1 Samuel 1–3 and 4–6 form a single text. The critical issue is how this is to be understood. In my judgement, both blocks of text prepare for the emergence of the monarchy, but in quite different ways.

1 Samuel 1–3 prepares the way for Samuel to step on to the stage of Israel's history as the prophet who would preside over the establishment of the monarchy in Israel. In my understanding, this aspect derives from the Prophetic Record.[25] The anti-Elide traditions were used as a foil to the presentation of Samuel; with a little help from the Deuteronomists, they also prepare the way for the new institution of monarchy by discrediting the old way of things. 1 Samuel 4–6, on the other hand, prepares the way for the emergence of the monarchy quite differently. The message of these chapters is entirely focussed on the ark, as the manifestation of God's power and purpose. In the withdrawal of the ark from the mainstream of Israel's life of worship, the way is left clear for new developments to occur. In the return of the ark to David's Jerusalem, under God's control of course, the seal of God's approval is placed on the newly established institution.

So I believe it is perfectly legitimate to speak of a text here. It is not a single sequence of sin and punishment. It is not a single text penned by one author; it is a composite text arranged by one author. It draws on the richness of Israel's traditions to portray the move toward the monarchy.

---

23. For my attempt to do this, see the *New Jerome Biblical Commentary;* contrast a different approach by Robert Polzin, for whom it is clear that chapter 4 is fulfilment of the prophecies in chapters 2 and 3 in all their dimensions (*Samuel and the Deuteronomist*, 60).

24. J Wellhausen, *Die Composition des Hexateuchs und der historischen Bücher des Alten Testaments*, fourth edition (Berlin: de Gruyter, 1963), 238.

25. For the Prophetic Record, see AF Campbell, *Of Prophets and Kings: A Late Ninth-Century Document (1 Samuel 1–2 Kings 10*, CBQMS 17 (Washington DC: Catholic Biblical Association of America, 1986).

1 Samuel 16–18

This is the well-known story of David and Goliath. Robert Polzin comments that it 'offers a serious challenge to anyone intent upon illustrating the narrative coherence of the present text'.[26] While admiring the courage of Polzin's effort with this text, I do not believe that he adequately spells out the full extent of the challenge, so I will endeavour to sketch it briefly here.

In 16:1–13, David, the youngest of Jesse's eight sons, is anointed by Samuel as Saul's replacement. As we know well, nothing more is heard of this anointing in the rest of the stories. In 16:14–23, Saul is in need of a lyre player to soothe his troubled spirits and David is summoned, enters Saul's service and becomes his armour-bearer as well as his lyre player. In chapter 17, we have the famous story of David's combat with the Philistine, Goliath. There are divergent text traditions in the Greek and Hebrew.[27] After the initial setting of the two armies in place, the giant Philistine champion comes forth to make his challenge to Israel: risk all in one-to-one combat with me! The reaction to the challenge is in v 11:

> When Saul and all Israel heard these words of the Philistine,
> they were dismayed and greatly afraid.

The Greek version continues with what is now v 32 in the present text. David, Saul's armour–bearer, speaks up from beside his king:

> Let no one's heart fail because of him; your servant will go and
> fight with this Philistine.

The sharp contrast between the dispirited Saul and inspired David is clear.

In the present text, however, v 11 is followed by v 12 which form-critically resembles a new narrative beginning. David is presented as Jesse's son, one of eight. This repeats information already given in 16:1–13. More significantly, it is a usual way to start an Israelite story.

---

26. R Polzin, *Samuel and the Deuteronomist*, 161.
27. In chapters 17–18, the shorter version common to Hebrew and Greek traditions is: 17:1–11, 32–40, 42–48a, 49, 51–54; 18:6a*b–9; 12a, 13–16, 20–21a, 22–29a; beyond this, the Hebrew alone has: 17:12–31, 41, 48b, 50; 17:55–18:6a*; 18:10–11, 12b, 17–19, 21b, 29b–30.

As a beginning, it would seem to be unaware of David's earlier role in the narrative. In v 15, however, it says that 'David went back and forth from Saul to feed his father's sheep at Bethlehem', indicating an awareness of David's place with Saul. It also notes in v 16 that the Philistine took his stand for forty days, morning and evening. This reflects an awareness of the earlier part of the David and Goliath story.

The story then takes its own independent way. Jesse despatches David to the camp with provisions for his brothers and a gift for their commander. The location of the Israelite camp is specified, as in v 2. The Philistine champion is brought on to the scene, introduced no more definitely than in v 4, and repeats his challenge, speaking 'the same words as before'.[28] The text adds:

> All the Israelites, when they saw the man, fled from him and
> were very much afraid (v 24).

We must wonder whether this flight and fear by all Israel was repeated morning and evening for forty days.

The story continues with the exchanges between David and the soldiery. Royal reward is promised for the one who will defeat this Philistine.

> The king will greatly enrich the man who kills him, and will
> give him his daughter and make his family free in Israel (v 25).

Form-critically, this is almost fairy-tale stuff: the youngest son, fresh from the farm, offered half of the kingdom and the hand of the king's daughter in marriage. David is portrayed taking up this theme and emphasising the issue of the reward to be gained. Finally the matter reaches Saul's ears and David is brought before the king. At this point, the two story–lines have converged, although for a while there is no more talk of reward.

At this point, it is time to pause and take stock. At first sight, we have two stories here: two introductions of David, of the battling armies, of the Philistine challenger. Is it possible to make sense of the

---

28. *RSV* and *NRSV* have 'a champion' in v 4 and 'the champion' in v 23. The difference in translation reflects the present text rather than the Hebrew; that is, the definite article is used in v 23 because it is the second occurrence in the present text, not because of any change in the Hebrew from v 4.

present text? We could appeal to the flashback technique, as legitimate in story as in film.[29] The narrative has brought the story to the point where King Saul quails before the menace to Israel's survival posed by the giant Philistine; David is about to face the menace and meet the challenge. But before we are allowed to hear David's response, then, the narrative takes us back to the origins of this brave man. So we see him coming from the farm to the camp, ready to be where he is now, brought by his bravery to Saul's side.

For Polzin, the opening description of the battle scene is expository (vv 1–11), with the exposition followed by the description of what happens at the battle scene when David actually arrives (vv 19–24). 'These two narrative sides of the battle scene are related to each other as exposition to story proper.' They are bracketed around the narrative introduction of David into the story (vv 12–18).[30]

The difficulty with this approach is that David has already been introduced into the story when he was brought to Saul's court and made his armour–bearer and lyre player. Even if David shuttled between his home and the court, a second introduction is not needed. The strongest argument against any harmonisation of the two passages is the continuation of the two stories, with noted differences at several key moments, and with fundamentally quite different themes. Harmonisation, as the key to understanding the text, founders on the repetition both of the killing and the question, 'Whose son are you?'

There is the moment of the killing. It is repetitive and different in the two versions. The version found in the Greek has David do the killing with a sword, after felling the Philistine with a slingstone.

> When the Philistine drew nearer to meet David, David put his hand in his bag, took out a stone, slung it, and struck the Philistine on his forehead; and the stone sank into his forehead, and he fell face down on the ground. Then David ran and stood over the Philistine; he grasped his sword, drew it out of its sheath, and killed him; then he cut his head off with it (vv 48a, 49, 51 [*NRSV*]).

The Hebrew verses which are absent from the Greek have David do the killing with sling and stone, there was no sword in David's hand.

---

29. David evokes his past when referring to his experience as a shepherd (17:34–36).
30. Polzin, *Samuel and the Deuteronomist*, 164–65.

> David ran quickly toward the battle line to meet the Philistine.
> And David prevailed over the Philistine with a sling and a
> stone, striking down the Philistine and killing him; there was
> no sword in David's hand (vv 48b, 50 [*NRSV*]).

While the two versions can be harmonised, there is a clear difference
in the presentation. If it were simply a matter of repetitive and full
detail, v 51 need only have read: And David ran and stood over him
and took his sword and cut off his head. There would have been no
need to repeat 'and he killed him'.

To clinch the matter, the two stories continue their separate ways,
pursuing quite different plots.

i.   The story of David, the armour-bearer and lyre player, after contrasting the dispirited Saul and the inspired David, follows this
contrast through with the song of the women and the success of
David, the jealousy of Saul, and the commitment of all Israel and
Judah to David (18:6a*–9, 12a, 13–16).

ii. The story of David, fresh from the farm and eager for a reward
from the king, continues with Saul's inquiries about David's identity ('Whose son are you?') and taking David into his service,[31]
the friendship between David and Jonathan, Saul's offer of the
hand of his eldest daughter Merab to David, and finally his failure to honour the offer, provoking enmity between the two men
(17:55–18:6a*, 18:10–11, 12b, 17–19 [21b], 29b–30).[32]

My point in going into this degree of detail about a well-known story
is to raise as clearly as possible the question: can this be a text? In my

---

31. Polzin recognises the difficulty here fully and frankly. He makes a valiant attempt
to construe Saul's 'Whose son are you young man?' (17:58a) as asking David
'formally to renounce Jesse's paternity in favor of his own' and to read as 'a note
of defiance' David's reply, 'I am the son of your servant Jesse the Bethlehemite'
(v 58b). Despite the ingenuity and insight, it just does not carry conviction (see
Polzin, *Samuel and the Deuteronomist*, 175).

32. For a fuller presentation of my interpretation of these stories, see my 'From
Philistine to Throne', in *AusBR* 34 (1986): 35–41 and my *Study Companion to
Old Testament Literature* (now Michael Glazier Books; Collegeville: Liturgical
Press, 1989), 206–13. Extensive treatment of the text traditions is given in D.
Barthélemy, DW Gooding, J Lust, and E Tov, *The Story of David and Goliath:
Textual and Literary Criticism*, OBO 73 (Fribourg, Switzerland: Éditions
Universitaires, 1986).

judgement, this text cannot be 'a text'. Attempts to unify its beginning by appeal to a flashback or differentiation between exposition and narration fail to do justice to the two clear and distinct storylines which are present. Does this then force us to adopt the position that its interpretation, as present text, would be an unsatisfying and embarrassing exercise? This may depend on how we understand the possibilities for interpretation of the text.

We have to reflect on the phenomena in the text and decide what kind of understanding will do the text most justice. There is no question of a covert appeal to the supposed crudity or clumsiness of redactors. If we do not have 'a text' here, we have the very skilled preservation of two texts, woven into a single narrative presentation. In my understanding, the phenomena of the text are best interpreted as an attempt to preserve two different stories, respecting their integrity and their difference. It is not to be understood as a attempt to compress and unify two stories into one. The differences have been maintained far too cleverly for that and could have been stamped out so very easily.

What the compilation has achieved here is to offer us two different visions of David's first moves to prominence and power. There is uncertain ambiguity in so much of the Story of David's Rise. Was it simply that God was with the David whom Samuel anointed? Or was there truth in Shimei ben Gera's taunts, 'Murderer! Scoundrel! Man of blood' (2 Sam 16:7–8). These two stories, at the beginning, leave avenues open to both views. David, the (anointed) armour-bearer and lyre player, is portrayed as the man who had God with him all the way to the throne. David, fresh from the farm and eager for a reward from the king, is more open to a portrayal as Shimei's ambitious and grasping scoundrel.

If the combined stories do not constitute 'a text', the outstanding question remains: why the interweaving here into a sequential text? It would have been perfectly possible to juxtapose them, as elsewhere in the Pentateuch or the Story of David's Rise (for example, 1 Samuel 24 and 26). On reflection, however, we can see the pitfalls involved in launching the royal career twice. Further, the difficulties encountered in interpreting the present text would be hugely multiplied if the two stories were told separately. Combined into a sequential text, all the details are available to a story–teller who then has the freedom to shape them as best befits the story to be told.[33]

---

33. See my 'Reported Story', above, note 16.

One of the interesting aspects of this David and Goliath story is that there appears to be an attempt to harmonise the two stories in the text itself. 1 Samuel 17:15 portrays David moving back and forth between his father's flock and Saul's court. 17:16 creates space for this by claiming that Goliath proclaimed his challenge morning and evening for forty days.[34]

Has such harmonisation succeeded? In my judgment, it has not. Close inspection shows that it fails.[35] But does that leave open a second way of reading the text in which we prescind from close inspection, a reading in which the unity of the text is foregrounded? We know that most unsuspecting readers of the flood story, the story of the deliverance at the sea, and the story of David and Goliath read these foregrounding the unity and leaving the issues of discontinuity unnoticed in the background. Once the critical perception of the nature of the text has been achieved, is there anything which disqualifies such a reading? I tend to think not. Such a reading is panoramic rather than close–up; it foregrounds unity rather than foregrounding diversity.

A panoramic reading can be greatly assisted by judiciously delimiting the text considered. If the David and Goliath story is begun at 1 Samuel 17:1 instead of 16:14, the tension with the David who is already in Saul's service is lessened. If the story is stopped at 17:54, the problem of Saul's ignorance of David's identity is avoided. For many purposes surely this is a legitimate procedure.

1 Samuel 7–12

The complexity of these chapters is well–known, with the claim to original texts, and prophetic and deuteronomistic overlays. To simplify brutally:

---

34. Such a forty day span would fit comfortably into the narrative horizon of the more legendary story as long as the motif of the flight of the troops was handled carefully—'All the Israelites . . . fled from him' lacks verisimilitude if repeated twice a day for forty days.

35. In fact, these two verses create considerable difficulties for close reading. Nevertheless it could be argued that since a modern scholar (for example, Polzin) believes the unity of the text can be sustained, the ancient compiler might have thought the same. While perfectly possible, if that were the case it may also be possible that both ancient and modern were wrong in their judgement.

- In 1 Samuel 7, God delivers Israel at Samuel's intercession by thundering mightily and throwing the Philistines into confusion (7:10).
- In 1 Samuel 8, the people demand a king in place of Samuel's sons, much to his displeasure, but he is instructed by God to set a king over them.
- In 1 Samuel 9:1–10:16, without any reference to this request, God acts to bring Saul before Samuel to be anointed king in order to deliver Israel from the Philistines—an action which is unnecessary in the light of thunderous divine power available through prophetic intercession.
- In 1 Samuel 10:17–27, despite having previously anointed him, Samuel uses oracular procedures such as the casting of lots to locate and identify Saul, in hiding, who is then acclaimed king.
- In 1 Samuel 11, a message reaches Saul, without any reference to his having been acclaimed king, and, empowered by the spirit, his military deliverance of a threatened town leads to his being crowned king at Gilgal.
- In 1 Samuel 12, most of this is pulled together, with an emphasis on Israel's sin and Samuel's continued prophetic intercession.

In a panoramic foregrounding of unity, much of the detailed disunity of these chapters can be overlooked. But is the pursuit of unity the best and richest way to derive meaning from them? Careful redaction has been at work with what result? Not a unified narrative by a long chalk. Nor is it an explicitly discursive text. Rather, we have the juxtaposition of differing traditions, with implicit possibility for the discerning of meaning between them.[36] There is conservation of at least one viewpoint, juxtaposed with contradiction or major modification from other viewpoints, resulting in communication of the varying views in Israel about the emergence of the monarchy.

I think it fair to say that a text has been constituted by the careful and unconcealed juxtaposition of differing positions. Such an inter-

---

36. Lyle M Eslinger comments: 'The existence of a text containing contradictory views should be assumed to present an examination of a controversy' (*Kingship of God in Crisis: A Close Reading of 1 Samuel 1–12* [Sheffield: Almond, 1985]. 38). Such an assumption seems to me thoroughly justifiable; Eslinger's scorn for a composite text stands in need of better justification than it gets. He manifests an appalling concept of historical critical interpretation (see 35).

pretation is justified in foregrounding the unity. The backgrounded diversity, not only between the blocks but above all within them, is immense and complex. I believe it is a fairer reading of the final text to recognise and respect the diversity, which has here been marshalled into line without being muted into unity.

Issues of meaning then and now

Turning to the question of meaning brings us within range of hermeneutic and literary theory. Without wishing to engage in the debates, there are certain elements worth a practitioner's while singling out.

The autonomy of a text is a gain since the days of Wimsatt and Beardsley which cannot be relinquished. As ED Hirsch notes, 'Self-evidently a text can mean anything it has been understood to mean. If an ancient text has been interpreted as a Christian allegory, that is unanswerable proof that it can be so interpreted.'[37] It is equally significant that we are able to distinguish between a critical construal of an ancient text and its anachronistic interpretation as a Christian allegory.

Our increasing awareness of the inevitability and value of subjectivity in all interpretation, as in so much else of human activity, prepares us to forgo the claim to *the* definitive interpretation of a text. Any interpretation I propose is my interpretation of the text, as informed and as responsible as I know how, as adequately and fully controlled by the text as I am able to make it. It is not humility but hermeneutic which renounces all claim to the definitive.

For the biblical believer, the autonomy of a text cannot be used universally to separate the interpreter's understanding of it from its origin as the word of God (however that might be spelled out). The historical or incarnational quality of God's word is essential to most Christian and Jewish belief. It is ultimately an issue of the nature of God's word: on the one hand, is it written in clear or in code; on the other, is it free of the trammels of human ambiguity or is it richly enmeshed in them? If association with an author and the distinc-

---

37. ED Hirsch, Jr, *The Aims of Interpretation* (Chicago: The University of Chicago Press, 1976). It is useful to remember Hirsch's distinctions between original meaning and anachronistic meaning, and between meaning and significance, and their various combinations.

tion between meaning then and meaning now are totally written off, the scriptures risk becoming either code or divorced from human involvement with God. Must either of these things happen?

If interpretation is always *my* interpretation, then it may be my interpretation of what it is appropriate for a text to mean now and my interpretation of what, in my best judgement, is appropriate for a text to have meant then, in the time of its composition.[38] The limits of my or our knowledge about 'then' may often mean that this aspect of interpretation is more negative than positive. That is, it may more often permit us to exclude meanings which we have reasonable grounds to be sure do not apply, rather than giving us reasonable and positive grounds to affirm a particular meaning. It is meaning controlled by my informed and responsible reading of the text, in the light of what I am able to know of its time. It may not and need not be identical with the anachronistic meaning which an informed and responsible reading of the text suggests to me as appropriate for today.

Today, in a post-critical world, I believe there is room for both critical and creative readings of the biblical text, each in its proper settings. We may signal these with antithetical balance. A critical reading will need to be informed and responsible, with particular reference to the time and context of the composition of the text, but aware of today. A creative reading will need to be informed and responsible, with particular reference to the time and context of today, but aware of the nature of the biblical text—and so post-critical. Today, a pre-critical reading would not be informed or responsible.

Hirsch argues that the decision between original meaning and anachronistic meaning is ultimately an ethical one.[39] The Bible was written, it is said, for the building up of the Jewish and Christian communities. Is it unethical for it to be read responsibly for this same purpose today?

Can the Bible be read as any other book? As incarnate word, can it be read in any other way? Yet it cannot be regarded as any other book, for the Bible is foundational for the faith-communities of Judaism and Christianity and that can be said of no other book.

---

38. It is not my recovery of the author's meaning, but my interpretation of the text's meaning.

39. Hirsch, *Aims*, 77.

Associated books:

Campbell, AF. *God and Bible* (Paulist Press)

Campbell, *Making Sense of the Bible: Difficult Texts and Modern Faith* (Paulist Press)

Campbell, AF, *Of Prophets and Kings* (CBQMS)

Campbell, AF. *Experiencing Scripture* (ATF Press)

Campbell, AF. *Joshua to Chronicles* (WJKP)

Campbell AF and O'Brien, MA. *Sources of the Pentateuch* (Fortress Press)

Campbell and O'Brien. *Unfolding the Deuteronomistic History* (Fortress Press)

Campbell, AF and O'Brien MA. *Rethinking the Pentateuch* (WJKP)

Rethinking Revelation:
The Priority of the Present Over the Past

Abstract

In most circles it has long been taken for granted that the composition of priestly material (P) in the Pentateuch dates to around the time of Israel's exile. With the more recent disintegration of the claim for a Yahwist (J), the trend in biblical circles is to see that the composition of non-priestly material in Genesis 1–11 could well have come from about the same time. It is difficult to date the composition of most ancestral texts much earlier than the book of Deuteronomy, around the late seventh century (see A Campbell and M O'Brien, *Rethinking the Pentateuch*, especially 22, Table 1). Close examination of two texts, Genesis 6:5–9:17 (the Flood) and Exodus 25–Numbers 10 (the Sinai sanctuary), allows the argument to be made that such texts do not portray how it was thought to have been back then, long ago, but rather how God is to be understood in the authors' day, the time of composition. The experience of their present determines how texts were written for ancient Israel. The experience of the present determines which texts are read by us today. Where revelation is concerned, because the practice of selective reading has existed for a long time, we change nothing in what we *do*. On the other hand, it may be necessary for much to change in what we *say* and *think*.

Preamble

With the exception of some solidly conservative biblical scholarship, the assumption is widely accepted that the present text of the Pen-

tateuch in its final form came together in post–exilic Israel. If most
of the priestly writing (P) is situated around the time of Israel's exile
(587–538), it is clear enough that the final form of the Pentateuch has
to be later. It should also be clear that the final form of the Pentateuch
was not compiled in terms of the age of the texts concerned, but in
terms of the chronology of their contents. The first chapter of Genesis, as text, is assumed to have been composed in the sixth century;
its contents require its being at the beginning.

Much of the book of Deuteronomy is generally dated to the seventh century, around the time of Judah's King Josiah. Deuteronomy
probably provides the earliest datable evidence for the traditions of
Israel's Pentateuch. It can be argued on solid grounds that, in the Pentateuch, for the most part, neither priestly (P) nor non-priestly (JE)
material is attested earlier than Deuteronomy. In the light of this, our
understanding of revelation may need rethinking. The purpose of
this paper is to explore the implications for our understanding of revelation confronted with the spreading acceptance in biblical circles
that little of Genesis–Numbers is significantly earlier than the period
around Israel's exile.

The initial moves toward this view have been in place for some
time. This paper explores a fraction of one possibility where these
implications are concerned. Discussion of Genesis 1–11 is restricted
to the Flood text; discussion of other texts is restricted to the Sinai
sanctuary. The paper falls into four parts: (1) a brief summary of the
theme; then the biblical core, (2) the Flood and (3) the Sinai sanctuary; finally, (4) a fuller discussion of the revolution in our understanding of revelation.

Preview

What is meant by 'rethinking revelation'? Once upon a time, by revelation we meant *what came from the past*, from the *word of God*.
Instead of this, the rethinking is to suggest that revelation for us
means primarily *what comes from the present*, from a *multiplicity of
influences*.

Despite appearances, many of the influences that impact on our
reading of the Bible as we articulate our thinking about God do not
come to us from the Bible itself but come to us from our reflection
on circumstances now. The legitimation for naming this revelation:

it is how the Bible was written. Such reflection, of course, takes into account the influence of the traditions that have shaped us.

We shape our understanding of Jesus quite differently, in dependence on the documents of that time. Our present may shape our reading of those documents; it does not diminish their role.

To return to the issue of our understanding of God and rethinking revelation. Israel's theologians pondered their present, reflected on their God, and produced their scriptures. We today ponder our present, reflect on our understanding of God, and then we select and read our Scripture in the light of this understanding.

The Flood text (Gen 6:5–9:17)

Beyond serious doubt, there are two relatively complete accounts of the Flood in Genesis 6:5–9:17. Naturally, we can smooth out passages here and there; the compilers who put the combined text together were competent operators. The reality of two relatively complete accounts, however, cannot be avoided. Given that two names are used for God, YHWH (personal name) and ELOHIM (common noun), one in each account, it is simple to designate the two as the YHWH-account and the ELOHIM-account. The high quality of their theology is remarkable; as remarkable is the theological difference between them.

To summarise swiftly, the principal differences between the two are: the names for God; the blocks of time; the nature and number of the animals; the origins of the floodwaters.

> In the YHWH-account, (1) the blocks of time are counted mainly as seven days and forty days; (2) the animals are both clean and unclean, seven clean and two unclean (probably pairs), and are described as 'the male and its mate'; (3) the origin of the floodwaters is from above ('the rain').

> In the ELOHIM-account, (1) the blocks of time are counted mainly as one hundred and fifty days; (2) the animals are undifferentiated as to ritual cleanliness ('two of every kind'), and are described as 'male and female'; (3) the origin of the floodwaters is both from above ('the windows of the heavens') and from below ('the fountains of the great deep').

In discussing the biblical Flood text, two points need highlighting here. First, the two accounts are notably different in their theological accentuation. Second, the theology derives from present knowledge not past revelation.

The YHWH-account begins with a real shocker. 'The LORD saw that the wickedness of humankind was great in the earth and that every inclination of the thoughts of their hearts was only evil continually' (Gen 6:5). Even after all the horrors of the last century or so, we could hardly put it more bluntly and brutally. That the wickedness of humankind has been great is beyond dispute; history leaves no doubt. The 'only evil continually' may be considered harsh, but is certainly true where large blocks of human activity have been concerned. God is not portrayed as angry, but as 'sorry' and 'grieved'. So God concludes: I am sorry that I made them; I will wipe out humans and everything else that lives. In the YHWH-account, it is only at this point, almost a postscript, that Noah gets a mention as finding favour in God's sight (6:8).

To the contrary, the ELOHIM-account opens with a couple of verses about Noah, as blameless and righteous and walking with God. It even mentions his sons (Gen 6:9–10). Then comes the judgement on the world, but—surprisingly—humans do not rate a mention. Instead of singling out humankind, the focus is on 'the earth' as corrupt and filled with violence, because 'all flesh' (which, of course, includes humankind) had corrupted its ways on the earth. Only then does the narrator have God tell Noah that there is going to be a flood to destroy 'all flesh'. (The phrase 'all flesh' is peculiar to this ELOHIM-account of the Flood, occurring eleven times between Gen 6:12 and 9:17; it occurs nowhere else in Genesis.) In this ELOHIM-account, God's opening speech ends with the covenant to be made with Noah (6:18), and the intention of preserving in the ark Noah's wife and children and the whole animal world.

These initial passages are avenues leading to two very different theologies—not accounts of past events but present theologies. In the first, the emphasis is entirely on the human race, seen as thoroughly evil. Noah is mentioned, late in the passage, as 'finding favour in the sight of the LORD'. In the text we have, nothing is said, about any ark or any lifesaving; we can assume something was there in the original YHWH-account. In the second, Noah's goodness is to the fore, the human race is lost sight of in the generic 'all flesh', and a covenant and the ark are explicit lifesavers.

What must not be lost to sight in all this is that the evil of human-kind and the corruption of all flesh *are not narrated*. They are assumed as evident; adequate evidence is not narrated. We will return to this.

In any telling of a flood story, the middle is relatively predictable. The floodwaters arrive; all aboard. The ark floats; the rest drown. The floodwaters subside; all ashore.

It is the ending of the Flood story that is a real surprise and that as biblical texts go is a brilliant piece of the most profound theology. Both stories are surprising.

The conclusion of the YHWH-account comes first. God is por-trayed alone ('said in his heart') and God is portrayed completely changing God's mind. For the same reason that God sent the flood in the first place (because of human wickedness), for that same reason (because of human wickedness), God will never do it again. The rea-son is given in almost the same words as it was at the beginning: 'for the inclination of the human heart is evil from youth' (8:21). It was a little harsher at the beginning (6:5): 'every inclination', 'only evil', and 'continually', a trace worse than 'from youth'. So, at the end, the verdict is softened a little; but the softening is slight. More surprising even than God's change of mind is the reality that in the narrative there is absolutely no evidence to support God's verdict. Noah and his family are just off the ark. All they have done is offer a sacrifice and its odour was pleasing to God. The evidence that 'the inclination of the human heart is evil from youth' (8:21) does not come from the story. As one possibility, it can come from Israel's experience of human living over the centuries. If so, the narrative is not about how things were back then, but about how things have always been, *from* the beginning until now.

The conclusion of the ELOHIM-account comes next (9:1–17) and is just as surprising. God talks to Noah and his sons. Under the new dispensation, the world they are to repeople will have 'fear and dread' resting on every animal (9:2) and, at the human level, murder and capital punishment (9:6). The surprise: with this less-than-perfect world, God is portrayed making an unconditional and everlasting covenant never again to destroy the earth with a flood (9:8–17).

The combined text, putting the two accounts together, helps to lessen God's unpredictability. The human wickedness of 6:5 and 8:21 is combined with the change of divine dispensation for the world. Unquestionably, God is portrayed having come to terms with a less–

than–perfect world. Human existence is not threatened by divine holiness. This is not a reflection on 'back then'; it is a faith claim for 'right now'.

The necessary combination of the two accounts has been very competently done. The horror of human evil is to the fore. The goodness of Noah is emphasised. The announcement of the Flood ends with the promise of salvation. In the YHWH-account, however, what happens at the end is not prepared for in any way—and cannot be. It is a total reversal on the part of God. In the ELOHIM-account, the ark, the covenant, and those in it prepare us to a limited degree for what is to follow. It is not to be a total reversal on the part of God, but a change in God's planning. The combined account does not shrink from the horror of human reality. The combined account emphasises that life will go on.

Here, in a double tradition, the All-holy is committed to the continued existence of the unholy—committed to humankind, to Israel, to us. It is the most profound theology, a theology of the human relationship with God. God is committed to us, unholy though we are. We are loved, sinners though we are. Right from the beginnings!

From the point of view of rethinking revelation, it is important to emphasise that in the biblical text there is absolutely no evidence to support God's verdict, at the end of the flood, that 'the inclination of the human heart is evil from youth' (8:21). This implies that despite the elimination of human life portrayed in the Flood and the affirmation of Noah's righteousness, there has been no change whatsoever in the behaviour of the human race. Noah and his family are just off the ark. All they have done is offer a sacrifice; its odour was pleasing to God. The evidence that 'the inclination of the human heart is evil from youth' (8:21) does not come from the story. As one possibility, it can come from Israel's experience of human living over the centuries.

What in the Bible's past came 'from Israel's experience of human living over the centuries', *in our present context* comes from our experience of human living in our own centuries.

The Sanctuary at Sinai (Exod 25–Num 10)

Israel's exodus from Egypt is easy enough to trace in the biblical text. There are two accounts of the call of Moses, two accounts of the plagues, two accounts of the Passover on the eve of Israel's departure, and two accounts of Israel's deliverance from the pursuing Egyptians at the Sea. Once past the Sea, a *single song* takes Israel all the way to Canaan (Exod 15). After Exodus 15, a *single itinerary* takes Israel to Mount Sinai; it is a priestly itinerary and would generally be regarded as relatively late. So, two accounts: (1) Israel gets into Canaan in Exodus 15; (2) on a different trajectory, Israel does not get into Canaan until the book of Joshua.

Following the second trajectory, we have Israel at Mount Sinai. Between the first two verses of chapter 19 and the last four verses of chapter 24, there are some five chapters of what we may term the 'Sinai capsule'. There is the theophany in chapter 19, the ten commandments in the first part of chapter 20, then some three chapters of the Covenant Code (20:22–23:32), and finally a covenantal ceremony and meal occupying most of chapter 24. We will not deal with this 'Sinai capsule' here. The reason is simple, if shocking. There is only one itinerary leading from the Sea to Sinai and it is in priestly language which is not the language of the 'Sinai capsule'. The narrative in the present biblical text does not get the Israel of the 'Sinai capsule' to Mount Sinai.

After Israel arrived at Mount Sinai in Exodus 19:1–2, passing over the 'Sinai capsule', we find in Exodus 24:15–18 that Moses went up on the mountain, the glory of the LORD covered the mountain for six days, and on the seventh day God called to Moses from the cloud and Moses entered the cloud and remained there for the next forty days. On the mountain, during those forty days, God gave Moses detailed instructions for the building of a sanctuary so that God may dwell in Israel's midst (25:8; 29:45). Once Moses has come down from the mountain, this sanctuary is built according to God's instructions, and is filled with God's glory (40:34).

The instructions given by God on the mountain are extremely detailed. First, there are the instructions for the sanctuary's equipment: ark of the covenant, table for the bread, lampstand, the tabernacle itself with its frame and curtains; there is also the altar, the court of the tabernacle, and the oil for the lamp. Second, there are instructions for the sacral vestments, ephod, breastplate, etc. Third are the instructions for the ordination of the priests. Following this, there are instructions for the daily offerings, for the altar of incense, the half-shekel sanctuary tax, the bronze basin, and the anointing oil and incense. Finally, the two principal workers are named, Bezalel and Oholiab.

Two features need to be noticed about this sanctuary, commanded by God on Mount Sinai.

- First, the sanctuary is portable. The ark of the covenant is made with rings and poles by which it is to be carried (25:14), so too the table (25:28), the altar (27:7), and the incense altar (30:4); the tent covering of the tabernacle is to be made of curtain units so constructed that it can be assembled to form one whole (26:11); the supporting framework is made of multiple units to be assembled according to the plan shown on the mountain (26:15–30). Other details need not detain us here.
- Second, the sanctuary is to be God's dwelling among the people of Israel (at the beginning of the instructions, 25:8; almost at their end, 29:45–46).

We need to have an idea of the detail specified to realise how important all this was to somebody. When Moses comes down from the mountain, six chapters are consecrated to the carrying out of the instructions in exquisite detail (Exod 35–40). The tabernacle is satisfactorily erected. 'The cloud covered the tent of meeting, and the glory of the LORD filled the tabernacle' (Exod 40:34).

Next follows the book of Leviticus, twenty-seven chapters regulating many aspects of Israel's moral, ritual, and sacrificial life before God in minute detail. Then comes the book of Numbers, with the first ten chapters devoted, among other things, to laying out in great detail instructions for the disposition of the camp and for the positions in the march away from Sinai. The camping order: Israel's tribes were to camp with the sanctuary in their middle. The marching order: Israel's tribes were allocated positions for the march with three tribes in the lead, three bringing up the rear, and two groups of three on either side, with the sanctuary in the centre.

Once again, two features need to be noticed:

- Probably at least three groups are involved in the composition of all this. The reason for emphasising this plurality is simple: if a number of groups were involved in this large complex of text, then a number of groups believed the whole enterprise to be important. Which leads to the second feature needing notice.

• Amazingly, this portable sanctuary, with its surrounding camp and protective order of march, leaves Mount Sinai and does not arrive at any definitive destination, not even the end of the first day. The detailed description of *departure* (Num 10:12–28) is nowhere followed by an equivalent description of *arrival*.

Because it goes against the grain for us to have Israel going no further than Sinai, even if only in this late tradition, it may help to add a detail or two. The departure, specified as 'for the first time' (10:13), takes place according to the planned order of march (10:14–27). At the end, it is noted simply: 'and they journeyed' (10:28; NRSV, 'when they set out'). In the centre of the march is the sanctuary. The tabernacle was taken down and carried by the Gershonites and the Merarites. The 'holy things' (we presume basically what belonged in the tabernacle) were carried by the Kohathites. The tabernacle was set up 'before their arrival' (10:21; literally, 'against their coming' [JPS]). The difficulty is glaring: they never arrive anywhere. They don't come. This whole massive sanctuary complex, to which some seventeen or so chapters have been devoted, goes *absolutely nowhere*. It starts splendidly; but the detailed description of *departure* (Num 10:12–28) is nowhere matched by any equivalent description of an *arrival*.

Conclusion

Regarding the Flood, a basic issue to be observed is *what is not narrated*, either at the beginning or at the end; namely, there is no narrative adequate to justify the charge of human wickedness.

At the beginning: in my judgement, the Flood text begins at 5:1, with verses 1–2 giving a succinct account of creation (differing slightly from Genesis One) and a ten-generation genealogy taking us down to Noah. No violence. If someone were to point to the earlier chapters with Adam and Eve, Cain, and Lamech, my reply would be simple. I do not believe that the disobedience in the Garden, the killing of Abel, and the intensification of violence associated with Lamech can possibly be considered adequate justification for the two statements: (1) that 'the wickedness of humankind was great in the earth', and that 'every inclination of the thoughts of their hearts was only evil continually' (Gen 6:5); and (2) that 'the earth was corrupt in God's sight, and the earth was filled with violence' (6:11).

At the end: there can be no question whatsoever that the narrative does not allow the slightest space for evidence to justify the statement that 'the inclination of the human heart is evil from youth' (8:21). The only humans on hand at the time are Noah and his family, Noah who has 'found favour in the sight of the LORD' (6:8) and who has been described as 'righteous' and 'blameless', walking with God (6:9).

Conclusion: the wickedness of humankind does not emerge from the narrative but is part of the narrator's present experience—as it is of ours. It is not a question of having been bad eggs in the distant past; it is the issue of being rotten eggs right up to now.

For the Sinai sanctuary, a basic issue is this: the sanctuary, so painstakingly described at Sinai, in the narrative *never moved* beyond the confines of the desert; furthermore, ancient Israel may well have known that no such sanctuary had ever arrived in Canaan. So why was so extensive a block of text consecrated to it. At least three reasons are possible: (1) it portrayed God as able to dwell in Israel's midst, independently of the Jerusalem temple; (2) it portrayed God as able to journey with Israel, guiding and controlling Israel's moves; (3) it portrayed God's presence in Israel's midst outside the land of Canaan.

The exiles of ancient Israel needed to believe that God could still dwell in their midst when the temple in Jerusalem was a smouldering ruin. The exiles of ancient Israel needed to believe that God could still journey with them, wherever that journey led and they needed to believe that God would guide and control their journey. The exiles of ancient Israel, exiled beyond their land, needed to believe that God could be present in their midst outside the land of Canaan. The priestly theologians who held firmly to these beliefs created an understanding of Sinai that took account of their present experience.

Does this stretch our imaginative faculties too far? The facts are there in the text of Exodus and Numbers; the sanctuary is lovingly detailed and goes absolutely nowhere.

Two parallels in the biblical text are well-known.

Leviticus 25 is devoted to the prescriptions, given by God to Moses, expressly at Mount Sinai, for the sabbath and jubilee years. We have no evidence that any such practice of the jubilee ever happened in ancient Israel, no expression of concern about failure to comply with it. It is a visionary idealisation, an imagined ideal, a theology expressed in law.

Ezekiel 48 has a geographical listing of the portions of territory allocated to each of the twelve tribes in Israel, north and south of the sanctuary. Nothing of the kind ever existed in ancient Israel. It is a visionary idealisation, a theology expressed in terms of a geographical vision.

Because the Sinai sanctuary goes nowhere in the text that prepares so carefully for it to go somewhere (right there is the signal to switch mindsets to *symbol*) and because such a sanctuary was not known in ancient Israel, I believe it too is a visionary idealisation, a theology expressed in terms of a sanctuary–centred vision.

The conclusion from all this: revelation does not come out of the past; its roots are in the present. The wickedness of humankind was not a revelation from the past; it was recognised in the present. God's capacity to journey in the midst of God's people was not a revelation from the past, but a reshaping of Israel's understanding of their God brought about by the needs of their present.

Briefly: for the biblical writers, their present shaped the way they understood their God and therefore how they *wrote* Scripture; for us, our present shapes the way we understand our God and therefore how we *read* Scripture.

To conclude: in terms of what we have been *doing* in our lives and our understanding of God, I am not at all sure that this rethinking of revelation changes anything much at all. I have no doubt that it changes enormously what we *say* and *think* about what we perceive ourselves doing. As such it is important because it requires us to be honest in our self-awareness.

We have always chosen what we appeal to from the Bible in proclaiming our understanding of God. Academics speak of 'a canon within the canon'. Whether such a view meets with appropriate approval as academic practice, in our day-to-day living it is unquestionably there.

When I say that this rethinking of revolution may not change much of what we do, I am claiming that the awareness of our present determines and has always determined what we select from Scripture and so shapes our understanding of God. What needs to be *said* then is that *this puts revelation for us in our present.*

God, Anger, and The Old Testament

Apart from a detour in defence of Job last year, my contributions to these gatherings have been focused on the appropriateness of the language we use when speaking about God. In 1985, I entered a plea for the right of the human analogy to be given full value as a paradigm for language about God: in a nutshell, it is unlikely to be appropriate or helpful to speak of God's action upon a human person in ways that could not be applied to the action of another human person. In 1986, I appealed to the story of David and Goliath for support in the understanding of a God who, rather than replacing human weakness with divine power, enables full human potential to be realized—a God who empowers human beings to use their talents and prowess in courageous and full living.

The topic of anger is irresistible for a person committed, as I am, to the Old Testament. The God of wrath is an all-too-common stereotype for the God of the Old Testament; the Old Testament's witness to an unshakably committed God, one might say an unconditionally loving God, is frequently overlooked. There is, therefore, a strong temptation to come to the rescue of the worth of the Old Testament and the reputation of its God, pointing out that, in the Old Testament, while Israel is frequently depicted as having broken the covenant which bound it to God and God to it, God is never portrayed breaking off the relationship with Israel. Only once, in Hosea, is God's message proclaimed as definitive rupture: 'You are not my people and I am not your God' (Hos 1:9). It is followed in the very next verse by the affirmation of restoration:

> And in the place where it was said to them, 'You are not my
> people', it shall be said to them, 'Sons of the living God'. (Hos
> 1:10)

Israel believed that God's commitment could be counted on, strong
words to the contrary notwithstanding. For example, in the book of
Judges, after a period of repeated infidelity, the narrator has Israel beg
for deliverance and can portray God replying:

> You have forsaken me and served other gods; therefore I will
> deliver you no more. Go and cry to the gods who you have
> chosen; let them deliver you in the time of your distress.

But Israel knew that this could not be God's final word, so the narra-
tor-theologian has Israel repent and God deliver them (Judg 10:13–
16). There is here a clear expression of faith in God's unshakable
commitment.

I am convinced of the value of the Old Testament's witness to a
deeply committed and trustworthy God, a God whose love is endur-
ing, a God whose love is robust enough to survive the buffets of
rebellion and rejection. As a result, for a long time my initial and
instinctive reaction to the association of anger with the God of the
Old Testament was to try and play down the anger aspect, countering
it with emphasis on the texts that highlight God's love. Over recent
years, I have come to realize that, if we believe in a loving God, we
can scarcely avoid belief in an angry God. In fact, it would be quite
intolerable to believe in a loving God without being able to use the
language of a deeply angry God.

Belief in God's love for every human being—not only ourselves,
but every individual on the face of the earth, in fact every person in
the long history of humanity—belief in such love has to go hand in
and with the language of God's powerful anger. Can one who loves be
anything but angered and furiously outraged by the suffering inflicted
on people by the willful or institutional callousness of other human
beings. When people died of starvation in Ethiopia or the Ukraine
because governments for political reasons deliberately directed food
supplies elsewhere, could a God who deeply loved those people be
thought of or spoken of in any other way than as deeply angered?
When people anywhere live in poverty and oppression because of
the apathy, greed, or prejudice of others, can one think of God as
genuinely loving these people without thinking of God as grieved

and angered? It is agony to think of the innermost being of God confronted by the Holocaust, the deliberate destruction of the Jews, God's chosen and beloved people. What commitment to human freedom could restrain God from action in such a situation? What fearful anger must have moved a loving God bound by such restraints? Or in the situations that are much closer to home, when someone acts coercively or selfishly toward another, we must speak of a loving God as grieved by the destructive behaviour of those who coerce and angered by the treatment meted out to those who are the victims of such violence, whether physical or more sophisticated.

It is important to give due place to this anger in God. Without it, the language of God's love has to be emptied of all emotional and passionate content—and the expression of passion in the Old Testament would have to be muted. Without it, what happens to us falls implicitly under the catch-all of divine providence and is understood to be willed or permitted by God to sufficient degree that it can leave God unmoved. If we shrink from using the language of God's anger, we run the twin risks of belittling God's love and burdening God with responsibility for all that befalls us.

Faith in the trustworthiness and lovingness of God, whether coming out of the Old Testament or the New, is immensely significant for an acceptance of the anger of God. We all know that the anger of a powerful figure inspires fear. Trust in a person's benevolence may make their anger tolerable; the certainty of a person's love makes it so much the easier to cope with their anger. When we have learned to trust God and to trust in God's love of us, it is easier to reflect on the anger of God—whether directed at others or directed at ourselves.

Most folklore about the Old Testament takes the primitive and angry behaviour of God for granted, without pausing to think about the nature of the sources. Some reflection, on the apparent manifestations of that behaviour in the Old Testament—even if very brief and incomplete—may be provocative of useful thought.

For example, God is believed to have commanded the extermination of Israel's enemies, every man, woman, and child. Sure enough, in 1 Samuel 15 there is a story in which Samuel gives God's command to Saul to go after the Amalekites:

> Now go and smite Amalek, and utterly destroy all that they have; do not spare them, but kill both man and woman, infant and suckling, ox and sheep, camel and ass (1 Sam 15:3).

Saul is reported to have done so, but with a couple of notable exceptions. He is in deep trouble with Samuel—and God—because he allowed himself to be persuaded to spare the best of the sheep and oxen, allegedly for sacrifice, and also because he spared the life of Agag, king of the Amalekites. Poor Agag, sole survivor of the Amalekites, did not last long. In holy fury, 'Samuel hewed Agag in pieces before the Lord in Gilgal' (15:33); a most unholy image—he chopped him up in church! My concern for the moment is simply to utter a caution against taking such a story too literally, either bemoaning the savagery of God or bewailing the fate of the late-lamented Amalekites. For fifteen chapters further on, the Amalekites are alive and well and plundering David's camp at Ziklag, taking captive the wives, sons, and daughters of David's six hundred men. When David struck back and caught them in the middle of a massive victory binge, despite David's being credited with wreaking most impressive havoc on the Amalekite forces, four hundred young toughs of the Amalekite camel corps are still around to escape (1 Sam 30:16–17). So much for the story about Saul!

Then there is the impression given in the book of Joshua that Joshua made a clean sweep of the country, killing everything that moved. As one verse sums it up:

> So Joshua defeated the whole land, the hill country and the
> Negeb and the lowland and the slopes, and all their kings; he
> left none remaining, but utterly destroyed all that breathed, as
> the Lord God of Israel commanded (Josh 10:40).

Joshua 11 concludes with Joshua having taken the whole land and given it for an inheritance to Israel according to their tribal allotments (11:23). Before we ponder this further example of apparently divine inhumanity, we need to take into account God's speech to Joshua in chapter 13 which asserts 'that there remains yet very much land to be possessed' (Josh 13:1), or Joshua's speech to all Israel in chapter 23 which warns against contact with the nations left in Israel's midst (Josh 23:7, 12–13), or the traditions in Judges 1 which enumerate all the cities Israel could not capture and whose inhabitants Israel could not drive out, or the differing traditions in Judges 2 which give various explanations of God's purpose in leaving many of the local inhabitants in the land (Judg 2:1–5, 20–23; 3:1–2, 3–6). So much for Joshua's campaigns of extermination!

A further aspect, which I find more difficult to deal with, is the threat uttered by the prophets that God was going to destroy Israel. It was no idle rhetoric; it was fulfilled. In the disastrous defeats of 722 and 587, Israel lost its status as a free and independent people, never to regain it until modern times. Yet as I struggle with the thought that God brought this upon Israel, I am well aware that Israel's decline and fall was brought about by the economic, military, and political factors of a small nation caught up in the struggle of empires. I am also well aware that the evils for which the prophets pilloried their contemporaries—basically, religious infidelity and social injustice—these evils of their own would have significantly contributed to the downfall of the people. Religious infidelity would have struck at the heart of Israel's sense of unity and purpose, and therefore at their strength of will to resist an aggressor. Social injustice would have eroded the morale and the will to fight of Israel's peasant army; conscripted peasants do not fight to defend the land which unjust laws and avaricious landowners have taken from them. So the anger of God against Israel is not divorced from the factors which destroy a people from within.

We cannot explore and explain all of this in one brief paper. It may be enough to say that the stories mentioned, and many more, are expressions of theology rather than records of history. They may be dubious expressions of a quite admirable theology—'obedience is better than sacrifice' (1 Sam 15:22), the land and Israel's life in it is God's gift (Josh 2–11). Or they may be expressions of theologies that are downright bad. But as bad theology they are less difficult than the historical reality of destruction and extermination. For our present purpose, it is enough to caution that before giving the God of the Old Testament a bad press for wrath and ruthlessness, it is extremely important to look closely at the evidence being alleged for conviction.

So far we have looked at the need to be able to attribute anger to God, and conversely the misunderstandings which give rise to the image of the Old Testament's angry God. I would like to conclude by turning to the issue of our anger directed against God.

The book of Job provides a canonical example of the open expression of anger directed at God. The benefits are evident, bringing suppressed feelings to a plane where they can be dealt with and generating a healthier and less fear-ridden relationship with God. Surely that is to the good. Yet I would be uncomfortable if this anger at God were seen as an end in itself.

My concern is twofold. Given our lack of direct sense-based experience of God, the question of where anger at God comes from is significant. A theologically inadequate understanding of our world can generate anger at God by attributing to God happenings for which God should not be held responsible. A theologically inadequate understanding of God can also generate anger at God by creating expectations which God is powerless to meet.

An unsatisfactory understanding of the world, too immediately involving God in its day–to–day happenings, hardly needs much elaboration. The person who attributes failure in an exam or loss of a job to lack of prayer needs to be angry at an inadequate theology rather than at God. The person who blames catastrophe on a punishing God—'What did I do to deserve it?'—is more the victim of inadequate theology than of God's justice.

Of greater concern to me is the second aspect, the one involving an unsatisfactory understanding of God. Anger at God can result from attributing a responsibility and omnipotence to God which may be quite unfair. Addressing the first of these Psychiatry and Religion conferences, I argued: 'If God's action upon the human person is best spoken of in terms of the mind and heart, the inevitable question must be faced of divine omnipotence.' I went on to say: 'In terms of language and the outlook it expresses, the common tendency is to speak and think in terms of the omnipotence of the all-powerful God; due reflection may suggest that God's respect for other persons can render God almost infinitely powerless.' This was greeted by a gale of laughter!

Yet it is an idea I believe we have to take very seriously. If it is right, a lot of anger against God would be misplaced. It is my belief that theological reflection and everyday experience point to a God whose overwhelming love sets such value on human freedom and integrity that God will never do violence to our human freedom. In many situations, therefore, God is powerless.

As I have argued in the early part of this paper, this powerlessness on God's part may well be the context for us to use a language of God's anger and frustration. The reverse side of this reflection is that language of anger on our part, directed against God, may well be inappropriate. The things that happen to us through the exercise of free will are outside the area of God's responsibility—they point rather to God's frustration and powerlessness.

The free will can be our own. We beg God to achieve some goal for us, but we do not ourselves take the steps necessary for its achievement. Anger at God would be inappropriate. The free will can be that of others. Our world is shaped by the behaviour and decisions of so many people, individually and institutionally. Some of the most wounding experiences suffered by people I have known have been inflicted on them by the actions of others. A loving God suffers with such people, is powerless at act with violence against the aggressor. Anger at God would be inappropriate.

We have to account for the apparent powerlessness of God to act in many situations in our world which seem to cry out for divine intervention. In my understanding, love excludes coercion and the perfect love of God is therefore powerless to coerce. However we explain it, the powerlessness of God removes the grounds for much of the anger that is directed at God.

There is, of course, the further realm of things which happen to us, independently of anyone's freedom. Examples are the accidents of birth, health, death, etc. Should we hold God responsible for these and so make God the butt of our anger? In my theology, no more than indirectly. If I may conclude by quoting from my own discussion of the book of Job:

> There is suffering in human life and we do not know why
> it should be . . . The denial of God does not alleviate the
> suffering one whit; all it eases is our inability to comprehend.
> Railing against God does nothing to help, unless it ventilates
> an anger that were better directed against the arbitrariness of
> misfortune.

Of course, we believe that it is God who created this universe in which we often experience either fortune or misfortune as arbitrary. So the problem remains at one remove—but the problem of evil will never simply go away. At least the recognition of the arbitrariness of misfortune places a distance between the responsibility of a loving God and our own experience of misery. It also leaves open the possibility that there is an overall value in the structure of our universe which is not visible in many of the individual situation we encounter. We have no guarantee that God created the best of all possible worlds, but we also have no way of knowing whether it was possible to create a better one (*The Study Companion to Old Testament Literature*, chapter 15, and fn 15).

The Nature of Biblical Narrative

Something of a paradigm shift has been in the making for a while in biblical studies. A future shape has yet to jell. The old historical-critical analysis has not been generating new life for a long time.[1] Other approaches have not so far struck lasting root. The interaction of developmental (cf diachronic) reading and interpretational (cf synchronic) reading is under way, but far from any agreed integration. A resolution of tensions between critical and literary approaches is still to be achieved. The factors involved in any shift are complex; among them, the often competing needs of faith communities, university communities, and so many competent individuals. One element in the total equation may be scholarly assumptions about the nature of much biblical narrative text.

Assumptions are unavoidable. We live with them all the time. Like routines, they help simplify life and eliminate the overburden of decisions to be faced at every turn. Like routines, assumptions can be dangerous; they can trap us in ruts we do not even realise. Those we are least aware of can be the most dangerous. Assumptions must be re-examined regularly; the outgrown need to be replaced.[2]

---

1. Herbert Hahn's comment was made over half a century ago: 'The conclusion seems to be unavoidable that the higher criticism has long since passed the age of constructive achievement' (*The Old Testament in Modern Research* [Philadelphia: Fortress, 1966; original, 1954] 41).

2. One of the great values of Susan Niditch's *Oral World and Written Word: Ancient Israelite Literature* (Louisville: Westminster John Knox, 1996) is that it seeks to bring to the surface some of our unconscious assumptions about literature and ancient Israel. Undoubtedly, some will feel that assumptions of little importance have been caricatured. Yet even caricature serves to challenge; and given what we know today of ancient Israel, it is time to reexamine and challenge assumptions. A recent study building on Niditch's work is Raymond F Person, Jr, 'The Ancient Israelite Scribe as Performer', in *JBL* 117 (1998): 601–9.

This article is about an assumption current in biblical studies that is a candidate for re-examination and replacement. The assumption concerns the texts of stories told in ancient Israel—the relationship between oral performance and written text.

Performance and narrative text

Appalling assumptions can sneak up on the greatest of scholars. Susan Niditch opens by upbraiding Hermann Gunkel for portraying a naive, child-like, rural simplicity as the culture from which the Bible emerged.[3] Alas, the same Gunkel did not do much better on the timing of biblical storytelling; it was much the same assumption that got him in trouble. In the introduction to his Genesis commentary, Gunkel seriously overestimated the time for the average biblical text. He notes that most of the Genesis stories comprise ten verses or so and they last, according to the first edition of the commentary, 'not much over half an hour'; in the third edition, this is reduced to 'scarcely a short quarter hour' (die kaum ein Viertelstündchen ausfüllen).[4] Unfortunately, Gunkel cannot have been driven by a desire for experimental accuracy. The Hebrew texts he mentions can mostly be read aloud slowly in two to three minutes each—a quarter hour is quite unnecessary and a half hour is an absurd overestimate (see below). It is all the more surprising, then, that Gunkel commented: the stories are strikingly short (*auffallend kurz*).

A couple of errors are running here for Gunkel. The first was factual: the length of the stories. The second is cultural: the people of ancient times were like our children. The factual error most probably

---

3. *Oral Word and Written Word*, 2.
4. The introduction to the first edition of Gunkel's *Genesis* (Göttingen: Vandenhoeck & Ruprecht, 1901) has been translated by WH Carruth, *The Legends of Genesis* (New York: Schocken, 1964; first published in 1901). It has the following: 'the older legends are absolutely abrupt to modern taste' and goes on to say that 'primitive times were satisfied with quite brief productions which required not much over half an hour' (47; 'etwa ein halbes Stündchen ausfüllen). This was corrected to a quarter hour in the second edition, 1902, noted by Jay A Wilcoxen ('Narrative', 57–98 in *Old Testament Form Criticism*, edited by John H Hayes [San Antonio: Trinity Univ. Press, 1974] see 64). The third edition reference, 'die kaum ein Viertelstündchen ausfüllen' is Gunkel, *Genesis* (Göttingen: Vandenhoeck & Ruprecht, 1910), xxxiv.

indicates an underlying assumption: the stories in the written texts either record or approximate to the stories as they were orally performed. The cultural prejudice allows the factual error to be accepted and the assumption to go unchallenged: ancient storytellers were not up to more complex stories and ancient audiences would not have sustained the listening needed. So the conclusion: the shorter a story is, the more likely it is to have kept its older form.[5]

To be fair to Gunkel, we need to be clear on the factual error. According to Gunkel, many of the Genesis stories hardly extended over more than ten verses. These are the stories that scarcely filled out a quarter hour.[6] What led one of the senior and highly respected exegetes of recent times into such a crass error? The most plausible explanation is that Gunkel worked with the assumption that the written text represented a record of the oral performance or a close approximation to it. No worthwhile story would be told in under thirty minutes; with Gunkel's view of an ancient Israelite audience, perhaps in around fifteen minutes—but no less. Yet the empirical evidence is that the 'telling' of ten verses of the biblical text takes on average less than three minutes.

Gunkel's failure to spot so egregious an error can be explained by the cultural prejudice. Gunkel attributes the shortness of the stories to the brevity of the attention span of ancient Israelite audiences. According to Gunkel, the stories are short because the attention span of the Israelite audiences was short. The truly patronising part is the assumption that the ancient Israelites were like our children (*so wie unsere Kinder*). A short piece was enough; after that, their capacity to listen was exhausted.[7] Today, I doubt that we have any difficulty in finding Gunkel's explanation totally unacceptable. He massively underestimated the abilities of an ancient Israelite audience. If the stories are as sophisticated as we have every reason to believe them to be, the audience is unlikely to have been less sophisticated.

Niditch is concerned with the reassessment of assumptions. She offers four scenarios for the relationship of text to performance.[8] They are:

---

5. 'Je knapper eine Sage ist, um so wahrscheinlicher ist es, daß sie in alter Gestalt erhalten ist' (*Genesis*, third edition, xxxiv).
6. *Genesis*, third edition, xxxiii-xxxiv.
7. *Genesis*, third edition, xxxiv.
8. *Oral World and Written Word*, 117–30.

i.   performance dictated and copied;
ii.   tradition written down by a gifted writer;
iii. literary imitation of oral style;
iv.   written composition from written sources.

Niditch highlights 'performance dictated and copied' for the classical prophetic corpus. 'Dictated and copied' may work for some prophetic passages; it does not work for narrative. The texts are too short; it would be Gunkel's fallacy all over again. Three minutes do not a story make. In Niditch's second scenario, the tradition has been formed by multiple performances and the possibility is allowed that 'written notes or abstracts aided the more elaborate performances'.[9] 'Notes or abstracts' may put us on track toward our present texts.

Almost seventy years passed before Gunkel's attitude was challenged by Alexander Rofé; even then, it was less the assumptions than the condescension that was objectionable. Without naming Gunkel, Rofé was justifiably indignant about a patronising attitude toward Israelite storytellers and listeners.[10] Around the assumption that the text records the performance, one sentence is key: 'The oral stage must have been longer, much longer, than the version we have now in scripture'.[11] According to Rofé, to look at the present written form of the stories as representing their form in oral performance would be the same as saying that the longest tale (of those he discusses) was narrated in about seventy seconds. When he went on a little later to

---

9.   *Oral World and Written Word*, 120.
10. Alexander Rofé, 'The Classification of the Prophetical Stories', in *JBL* 89 (1970) 427–40. His indignation needs to be heard (432–33).

     Yet are we allowed to consider the present form of the stories as their original oral form? This would amount to saying that the longest tale was narrated in about seventy seconds, implying that the storyteller could not entertain his audience any longer than that and that the audience itself would be satisfied with such a short, concise, matter-of-fact account. This, however, is highly improbable. The Israelite storyteller was not a primitive who could not even master his language, and the Israelite public was not so backwards as not to be able to sustain a story which lasted more than one minute. The oral stage must have been longer, much longer, than the version we have now in scripture. The conciseness of the present stories rather reveals the opposite: the man who reduced these narratives to writing took the pains, and had the skill, to condense them.
11. Rofé, 'The Classification of the Prophetical Stories', 432.

discuss 'a very different type of story', one that was 'much longer (30 verses)', Rofé passed over the significance of what he had been saying, although much more than length was at issue.[12] Thirty verses might occupy about ten minutes, in serious storytelling terms about as inadequate as seventy seconds.

Almost in passing, Gunkel's error was targeted a little later by Jay Wilcoxen, but without noticeable impact on subsequent scholarship.[13] Wilcoxen suggests

> that Gunkel may have missed the point of the brevity of the present texts. The individual stories are not brief because ancient narrations were brief, but because these texts only present basic plots which in any actual narration would be expanded and elaborated according to the skill of the storyteller and the occasion of his performance.[14]

In an article a few years earlier, Wilcoxen had argued that Joshua 6 preserved three forms of ritual, merged to retain the legitimacy of all three. He comments: 'On any single occasion, however, only one of the forms must have been selected.'[15]

Without reference to the work of Rofé and Wilcoxen, Antony Campbell argued in 1989 for understanding some texts as reported story, 'the outcome of reporting what a story is about'. A reported story would provide 'the basic elements from which the full narrative of a story can be developed but would fall short of actually telling the story'.[16] The idea has been taken up subsequently by Campbell and O'Brien.[17] Their emphasis was on the text as base for later storytell-

---

12. Rofé, 'The Classification of the Prophetical Stories', 433.

13. Wilcoxen, 'Narrative', 64–66.

14. 'Narrative', 65.

15. Jay A Wilcoxen, 'Narrative Structure and Cult Legend: A Study of Joshua 1–6', 43–70 in *Transitions in Biblical Scholarship*, edited by JC Rylaarsdam (Chicago: University of Chicago Press, 1968), 53.

16. Antony F Campbell, 'The Reported Story: Midway Between Oral Performance and Literary Art', in *Semeia* 46 (1989): 77–85, 78.

17. Antony F Campbell and Mark A O'Brien, *Sources of the Pentateuch: Texts, Introductions, Annotations* (Minneapolis: Fortress, 1993) and *idem*, '1–2 Samuel' and '1–2 Kings' in *The International Bible Commentary*, edited by WR Farmer, *et al* (Collegeville: Liturgical Press, 1998), 580–81; restated in *idem*, *Unfolding the Deuteronomistic History: Origins, Upgrades, Present Text* (Minneapolis: Fortress, 2000) 6–7.

ing. Niditch's second scenario, the tradition written down by a gifted writer, points to a correlative aspect of such reported stories—they emerge from the tradition of Israel's storytelling.

Past traditions and future telling

As a result of these observations, another scenario needs to be added to the four proposed by Niditch. Many of the narrative texts we have in the Bible stand in an indirect relationship to the performance of storytelling. They are too short to be stories as performed; beyond that, many of them are not appropriate for that purpose. Instead, these biblical texts look in two directions: one is rearward, back to the storytelling tradition that they report; the other is forward, to the stories to be told in the future.

The rearward glance, the report of storytelling tradition, is close to the second scenario depicted by Niditch (with the added aspect of reporting and reduction).[18] We know the texts we have and the high quality of their literary style; it is a tribute to the quality of ancient Israel's storytelling. Those who told the stories told them well; those who reported the stories reported them well. The plot structure is there. The gems of dialogue are there. The details that go to make a good story are there. There is enough stuff there to hold a report together. The trimmings that any good storyteller can generate are not there. Variant versions are there, even if only briefly noted. A storyteller may choose to use one; no good storyteller would actualise conflicting ones. Contradictory traditions are sometimes noted. Good storytellers knew how to handle them. Fundamentally, a good report preserved whatever possibilities the tradition contained. The aim of a reported story is to recapitulate the story—not to retell it but to recapitulate it.

The reported story is then a base for the storyteller whose task is to retell the story. Choices may be made from that base: which variants to tell, which details to include. A good storyteller will know, on any given occasion, which details to provide and which to withhold, which gaps to fill and which to leave as gaps. A good storyteller will

---

18. The emphasis on the rearward aspect, the derivation of the reported stories from the practice of Israel's storytelling, emerged for me from discussions with Professor Marvin Sweeney.

know when to extend a story and when to shorten it. The base may contain several variants; the good storyteller will only actualise one and will know which is the right one to actualise for the particular audience. It is not a matter of being bound to a text but being bound to a story. The reported story preserves a past tradition, rehearsed in the telling of the story, and prepares for a future rehearsal of the tradition, in the retelling of the story. There is a structured move here from the oral into the written with a view to returning to the oral.[19]

We have no certainty that reported stories functioned as bases for storytelling. That is an assumption, although it is an assumption that is grounded in verifiable argument, is respectful of ancient writers, and is free from patronising elements. The principal grounds of argument for regarding certain texts as reported stories may be summarised under three heads:

i.   the brevity of the texts, as discussed above;
ii. the details omitted, requiring a fuller discussion than space allows for here;[20]
iii. the variants included, often to be accounted for as elements or traditions preserved for the consideration of later storytellers and later generations.[21]

The story texts we now have belong mainly in the Pentateuch, the Deuteronomistic History, the Chronicler's history, and some in the prophetic books. Calculating on the average of three minutes or so for ten verses, the record of an hour-long performance of a story would require a couple of hundred verses. The narrative texts of the Bible would be some twenty times more extensive than they are. Not twenty Bibles, but quite a number. Some reduction of the traditional performances of stories was needed to give us the extended texts we

---

19. This reinforces Niditch's important insistence on the influence of oral culture in a world of limited literacy.

20. To cull three examples from one chapter: messages are acted on without being delivered (1 Sam 19:14); people are present in a place without having gone there (19:17); elements of a story are not plausible without a level of explanation that is not given (19:15–16, where the dummy is used too late).

21. The space available does not allow for full discussion. Among other research, these observations are based on preparation of the *First Samuel* and *Second Samuel* volumes for the Forms of the Old Testament Literature series (forthcoming with Eerdmans, Grand Rapids) and on the works listed above in notes 16–17.

have. In this case, there is no assumption. We have the reduced texts. The only assumption made is that stories were told before they were reported—that performance preceded report.

The story texts of the Older Testament range from a verse or two to fifty or sixty verses. Some of these texts read well in church; but the synagogues of ancient Israel came long after the stories. A few of these texts could well have been used at the festivals of ancient Israel; they are relatively few however. Most are not suitable for festival use. The settings were almost certainly not simple; they range across the gamut from entertainment to theology. Two claims can be made. First, these reported stories were used to compile the extensive narrative documents that are part of the present biblical text. Second, it is a reasonable assumption that these reported stories served as the bases from which continued storytelling was launched in ancient Israel.

Biblical narratives are often familiar texts, sacred texts, treasured texts. It is difficult to look at these texts differently, yet difference may not mean loss and the beneficial implications may be considerable.

In a classic study, Erich Auerbach comments that Hebrew narrative is 'fraught with background'.[22] For example, Auerbach points out that the sacrifice of Isaac (Gen 22) starts without any divine journey or divine council. Yet, as we are well aware, Israelite narrative knows of both: in Genesis 17, God journeys (God appears to Abraham and goes up from him); in 1 Kings 22, we are privy to the proceedings of the divine council. But not in the text of Genesis 22.

Auerbach's comparison of the Older Testament with Homer is an important starting point. Comments from his conclusion to the chapter on 'Odysseus' Scar' are worth repeating.

> The two styles, in their opposition, represent basic types: on the one hand [that is, Homer] fully externalized description, uniform illumination, uninterrupted connection . . . all events in the foreground, displaying unmistakable meanings . . . on the other hand [that is, the OT], certain parts brought into high relief, others left obscure, abruptness, suggestive influence of the unexpressed, 'background' quality, multiplicity of meanings and the need for interpretation . . . [23]

---

22. E Auerbach, *Mimesis: The Representation of Reality in Western Literature* (Princeton, NJ: Princeton Univ. Press, 1953; original, 1946), 12.
23. *Mimesis*, 23.

Auerbach's reading of the Older Testament is marked by orthodoxy and piety. In his view, the sole concern of the biblical stories is with moral, religious, and psychological phenomena. Furthermore:

> Their religious intent involves an absolute claim to historical truth . . . The Biblical narrator was obliged to write exactly what his belief in the truth of the tradition . . . demanded of him . . . his freedom in creative or representative imagination was severely limited; his activity was perforce reduced to composing an effective version of the pious tradition.[24]

A different experience of the biblical text denies this limiting of the biblical narrator to the composition of an effective version of the pious tradition. This is a far cry from Robert Alter's 'historicized prose fiction'.[25] For all that, Auerbach's 'fraught with background' has caught something characteristic of Hebrew narrative text. What is the significance of this characteristic within the texts? Is it possible that Genesis 22, for example, is a reported story or a story base? It has all the makings of a most powerful story, but as the text stands the story takes about four minutes to tell. It is a brilliantly shaped literary text; it need not reproduce the performance of storytelling.

Would it spoil this story if, in its telling, a storyteller mentioned God's coming down to speak to Abraham? Would it spoil this story if a storyteller allowed a glimpse into the proceedings of the divine council so that an audience might be more informed as to God's purpose? Would it spoil the story to introduce Sarah (cf Genesis 21)? Would it spoil the poignancy of the dialogue of father and son about the victim, as 'the two of them walked on together' (vv 7–8), if a little bit of storytelling attention was given to the strained silence that might have preceded Isaac's question or if Abraham was allowed to give his son some inkling of what was at stake? The text ignores Isaac. What if the issue of Isaac's return with his father was raised by the storyteller? In the text it is a gap. In all the gaps and the silences, we have to ask how this brief text functioned. It is a brilliant literary text. Is it a brilliantly reported story, a base for equally brilliant storytelling?

---

24. *Mimesis*, 14.
25. R Alter, *The Art of Biblical Narrative* (New York: Basic Books, 1981), 24. The term itself is taken from Herbert Schneidau's *Sacred Discontent*.

Social conditions

Economist Maynard Keynes is reputed to have said that people who claimed they had no need of economic theory were simply in the grip of an older theory. It tends to be the same with assumptions. Older assumptions do not easily release their grip. We cannot avoid assumptions about how an ancient society functioned, what went on in a society where literacy was highly restricted, what sort of a literary industry gave rise to our Bible texts. We make those assumptions best if we project off knowledge of similar societies rather than re-tro-jecting our own prejudices. All this makes Niditch's book immensely valuable.[26] At the same time, in biblical studies we have to square our assumptions with the biblical text. The hypotheses and social conditions we assume need to be the sort that would bring about the texts we actually possess. Wise generalisations are of no use to us if they do not shed light on the texts we look at in their detail. The modern recovery of antiquity is extremely important, but hypotheses have to be measured against the texts they supposedly produced.

If modern study is not totally wrong—and it may be—there is an intensity of editing in the priestly documents and the deuteronomis-tic texts. We know about parties and factions in the ancient world. We do not know the details of how these swirled in and out of royal courts or sacred temples or established families (for example: we can trace three generations of Shaphans in Jerusalem, from Secre-tary Shaphan ben Azaliah ben Meshullam [2 Kgs 22:3] to Governor Gedaliah ben Ahikam ben Shaphan [2 Kgs 25:22; Jer 39:14; 40:5, 9, 11; 41:2]). The intensity of factional partisans need not correlate with their influence in society. I recall the words of an American candidate for presidential nomination: 'I am not bound by the party platform; I have not even read it.' I doubt that such a disavowal did much to stop infighting over the platform. Were similar passions at work in priestly and deuteronomistic circles? The texts suggest it. Where were such circles and their texts housed? Were they institutionally based? We do not know. We have only the texts and their characteristics that we must account for.

---

26. Particularly chapter 3 ('New Ways of Thinking about Orality and Literacy: Israelite Evidence') and chapter 4 ('Logistics of Literacy: Archives and Libraries, Education, and Writing Material').

Examples

Leaving the Pentateuch aside, when we start scrutinising texts using the 'reported story' concept as a lens for reading, examples are legion. The crossing of the Jordan text (Joshua 3–4) makes much more sense as a base story that has been annotated with liturgical options instead of an unconvincing weaving of incomplete traditions. The text of the fall of Jericho (Josh 6:3–20) lacks plausibility as present text or a combination of sources. It makes sense as a script suitable for story-telling or liturgy, either suspenseful and silent (Alfred Hitchcock) or showy and noisy (Cecil B de Mille).[27] To pull a couple of texts out of Judges, Jephthah's is a story that might be told of a hero empowered by the spirit (Judg 11:29) or of a warrior who made a stupid vow and stubbornly stuck to it (Judg 11:30–31). These are options for a story-teller. Samson's too is a cycle that offers a storyteller multiple options. Samson 'shall begin to deliver Israel' (Judg 13:5). Which will get the emphasis: the beginner or the deliverer? Samson is scarcely a hero figure.[28] With Delilah, for example: three times he is deceived, three times he has lied. Smart. The fourth time he has to know that he will be deceived; this time, he tells the truth. Not smart. No theological nobility either; savage selfishness instead: 'So that with this one act of revenge I may pay back the Philistines for my two eyes' (Judg 16:28). What a contrast with David facing the Philistine (1 Sam 17:45–47).

David and the Philistine champion offers a good example of the storyteller's need either to choose or to demonstrate remarkable mental agility (1 Sam 16:14–18:30). There is a choice between David the armor-bearer, acting out of lofty theological faith (17:36–37, 45–47), or David the shepherd-boy, acting out of raw ambition (17:26). The present text hints at combining the two. A skilled storyteller might be able to do it, but it would demand no little agility. A storyteller's development of the text base is needed for the story of David and Saul in the cave (1 Sam 24). The present text has David emerge from the cave, waving the corner of Saul's cloak, while three thousand of Saul's

---

27. See the treatment of both passages in *Unfolding the Deuteronomistic History*, 112–17 and 119–23.

28. Gerhard von Rad comments: 'The oddest figure amongst the judges is Samson: the reader will indeed find it absolutely impossible to understand him as judge over Israel' (*Old Testament Theology*, [2 volumes; Edinburgh: Oliver and Boyd, 1962–65] 1.333).

finest look on. A storyteller could easily have David discuss the situation with his men in the cave, slip away through a gully behind the cave, and call to Saul from concealment in a section of forest higher up the hill. The text does not. The text also has David's moral stance in the cave come a verse or two too late (24:4–7). It is an option for the storyteller, not a plot development in the text. The chapter is not the telling of a story but its report, the base for storytelling. The narrative of how David rose to power in Israel is a composition of some twenty-five to thirty-five stories, brilliantly woven together and provided with the necessary narrative thread. Almost all of them are candidates for a storyteller's enhancement. Almost all of them, some more evidently and others less so, are candidates for reported story status—are too short or too multiplex to be anything but bases for storytelling.

The stories of 2 Samuel 11–20 are renowned for the issues they raise and the gaps they leave.[29] These chapters may have served their purpose as literary texts. They are also wonderful bases for storytelling. In the case of Bathsheba and David, for example, a storyteller might choose to note whether Bathsheba's washing was unduly revealing or not and whether it mattered. The text is silent (2 Sam 11:2). A storyteller might reflect on Bathsheba's feelings going to or returning from David's palace. The text is silent (11:4). A storyteller might have spent time on why she sent the dangerous message, 'I am pregnant', and what David's options might have been. The text is silent (11:5–6). And so many more. When Absalom's revolt is announced, David takes flight from Jerusalem without a word of counsel. What became of the claim for the impregnable city that 'even the blind and lame will turn you back' (2 Sam 5:6)? The text is silent. Hushai's runners hid in a well at Bahurim (2 Sam 17:15–20). Details of why it was risky for them to be seen and how Absalom's people knew to search the house at Bahurim are not given. A servant girl has been introduced as an apparently regular courier (17:17); the present text leaves no time for any such repeated activity.

Rehoboam's loss of the north invites development (1 Kgs 12:1–20). Were the young counselors greedy? Were the old wise? How was God's will at work? A choice is forced on the storyteller: was Jeroboam called to Shechem before (v 3) or after (v 20) the political

---

29. M Sternberg's treatment of gaps is classic (cf chapter 6 of *The Poetics of Biblical Narrative* [Bloomington: Indiana University Press, 1985], especially190–222).

split? In 1 Kings 21, a storyteller might have focused on the responsibility of either Ahab or Jezebel, or might have combined the two more thoroughly. The text leaves the options open (vv 1–16) and includes multiple traditions in vv 17–29. 2 Kings 3 mingles water and war, victory and retreat, two kings or three. A storyteller faced choices or development. In 2 Kings 13, King Joash is buried in v 13 and visits the dying Elisha in v 14; the regnal formula for Joash is given at 13:12 and repeated at 14:15. There is storytelling material in between, not necessarily edifying. The text presents it; a storyteller could have chosen how to handle it.

Multiplying examples will simply take us through most of the storytelling texts of the biblical tradition. The brevity of the texts and the nature of the texts combine to make a powerful case for the movement from oral to written to oral—the reported story recapitulates the oral performance, can be integrated into one of Israel's longer narrative compositions, and can serve as base for future retellings of the tradition.

Conclusion

These observations on the reported story have a radical impact on our understanding of the nature of biblical text. They impose caution on critical analysis of the text. They enhance access to the literary qualities of the present text. They give scope to creativity and flexibility in the interpreters of old and of today.

Access to the present text is not constrained by the need to find everything within the text itself. When the text recapitulates a story or is a base for a future story, the freedom left to the ancient storyteller is also there for today's interpreter. The control exercised by the text is not abolished but is altered. The written text is no longer the whole story, but it captures the nature of the story. If it offers options, like the storytellers of old we too know what they are. The option has always been there for us to accept or to reject. The choice may now be widened.

The literary quality of the text is not diminished by recognition of its status as reported story. A high tradition of storytelling leads to a high tradition of reporting and serves to foster equally high standards in the future. Many of our narrative texts are respected as highly polished works. We have no reason to believe that those who created the written text of reported stories did not take a pride in their literary achievement. Gaps left in the text need not be filled by the storytellers, ancient or modern; if we leave them unfilled, we know that we leave them because of the value of the gap. Shades of meaning in the choice of vocabulary are shades of meaning that any worthwhile storyteller would take over into the story. Insights into character preserved by the text are insights to be developed in the storytelling. And so on.

Texts that preserve options and retain contradictory traditions are responsibly respectful of the traditions of ancient Israel. It is one of the wonders of the Israelite scriptures that they offer so rich a palette of contrasting views. Whether it is creation, exodus, wandering, conquest, monarchy, or divine providence confronted with human suffering, Israel's contrasting views are preserved in its scriptures. Even in the traditional self-description of God, tension is maintained: 'forgiving iniquity and transgression and sin' (Exod 34:7a); 'by no means clearing the guilty, but visiting the iniquity of the parents upon the children' (Exod 34:7b). Israel offered choice to its theologians and to its storytellers. Today the biblical texts still offer us choices.

Job: Case Study or Theology

It was a friend who practises both as psychologist and biblical scholar who pointed out to me that the encounter with a text proceeds on much the same lines as the encounter with a person. I suspect an academic approaches a book in much the same way that a psychiatrist approaches a client. You want a history from a client. So do we from a book. Where did the author study and under what scholars? What is the background to the book: doctoral dissertation or years of mature study? What problem is the client presenting? What insight or impulse drove the author to write this book? What are the client's circumstances and resources? Who has the author been reading, talking to, working with? The comparison can be pushed quite a bit further, but that is enough for present purposes.

It was a psychiatrist friend who first loaned me a recent book in the Gaskell Psychiatry Series, entitled Job's Illness: Loss, Grief and Integration. A Psychological Interpretation, by Dr Jack Kahn.[1] A glance at the Introduction showed training in medicine and psychiatry. A glance at the Bibliography showed half a dozen translations of the Bible, four entries under Bible Commentaries, nineteen entries on matters Literary, Philosophical and Historical (none of which were seriously biblical), and fifty-seven entries on matters Medical, Psychiatric and Psychological. I restrained my initial impulse to condemn Jack Kahn for hubris, reflecting that what matters is not how many books you read but how well you choose what you read. Had he chosen his commentaries well?

---

1. Jack Kahn with Hester Solomon, *Job's Illness: Loss, Grief and Integration: A Psychological Interpretation*. Gaskell Psychiatry Series (London: The Royal College of Psychiatrists, 1986).

The titles were not encouraging. Bible Commentaries and an Encyclopedia, but no commentaries specifically on the Book of Job. The dates were even less encouraging: 1839, 1902, 1919, and—a little more up-to-date—1947. Regrettably, as far as the date was concerned, the 1947 offering turned out to be that great classic, *The Guide for the Perplexed*, by Moses Maimonides, dating from 1168. With some indignation, I then wondered what utterly unenlightened press might, in this twentieth century, have published a book on Job, garnished with some of the trimmings of an academic bibliography, but with practically no consultation of any worth-while scholarship on the Book of Job since Maimonides in the twelfth century. Imagine my shock to discover that my unenlightened publisher was no less august a body than the Royal College of Psychiatrists.

There is a value in being open to surprise, as well as to others' eccentricities. Who knows, freedom from knowledge might generate freedom for helpful insights. But I was not immediately attracted to explore Dr. Kahn's contribution. There was not even a disclaimer somewhere to indicate that he was aware of the importance of what he was ignoring. Ah well, his book could wait for some unlikely moment of idle leisure. But the fates were against me. A second psychiatrist friend gave me a copy. My reaction—gratitude apart, of course—was one of mild horror: My God, psychiatrists are buying this! They may even read it! Then came Dr Chiu's invitation to present a paper to this conference. So that did it. My paper had to address the question whether Jack Kahn's exploration of the Book of Job was legitimate.

The basic issue

I do not want to cast myself in the role of the professional scholar jealously defending specialist territory against the intrusions of well-meaning amateurs. The Book of Job is a work of literature and a classic. It is not burdened with the peculiarities of history and composition which can make some biblical books minefields for the uninitiated. So why should I entertain reserves simply because Jack Kahn's bibliography is hugely out of balance? In this paper, I am waving a yellow flag of caution about a particular book by a particular psychiatrist who is trespassing on my professional turf. I do so because there is a very delicate flower concealed in that turf, and it would be a great pity to trample on it without being fully aware of what we are doing.

The basic problem inherent in Kahn's undertaking is reflected in the conflict between the beginning and the end of his first chapter. At the beginning, he quotes from Maimonides, who refers to:

> the strange and wonderful Book of Job [whose] basis is a fiction, conceived for the purpose of explaining the different opinions which people hold on Divine Providence . . . This fiction, however, is in so far different from other fictions that it includes profound ideas and great mysteries, removes great doubts, and reveals the most important truths.[2]

The chapter concludes:

> From a purely psychiatric point of view, it is possible to find in the Book of Job a sensitive and detailed account of the onset, course, and treatment of a mental disorder in which the most prominent feature is depression . . .
>
> The purpose of this book is to study the illness and the events surrounding it, and to find in the Bible story an account of some of the universal problems of mankind as revealed through critical events in the life of one individual. It is also concerned with the progression of ideas of human identity and the way in which human beings have searched for a harmony between experience of the self and experience of the universe.[3]

There are two things seriously wrong here, and Jack Kahn skates far too lightly around one and does not seem to be aware of the other.

If Maimonides is right that the Book of Job is a fiction—and modern scholarship would agree with him—and if we take seriously that it presents itself as a third-person narrative about Job, the bulk of which is high flown poetry presented as the speeches of Job, then we must be cautious about finding in it 'a sensitive and detailed account of the onset, course, and treatment of a mental disorder'. Firstly, the account is not from the patient, but from an author—and a poet to boot. Dr Kahn does not have access to 'critical events in the life of

---

2. Kahn, *Job's Illness*, 1–2, quoting from Moses Maimonides (1168), *The Guide for the Perplexed*, translated by M Friedlander (London: George Routledge & Sons, 1947), 296.
3. Kahn, *Job's Illness*, 12.

one individual'. He has access to a third party's poetry. Surely this is significant for the legitimacy of using this ancient text as a subject for psychiatric analysis. If what we have are the words of a person describing their own experience, some validity would have to be allowed to attempts at interpretation or analysis. But when the words are put in a character's mouth by an author, we have only the product of creative imagination; there is not the control of present or remembered personal experience. One might always argue that an author must build on some analogous experience—but surely the process is fraught with difficulties and dangers. The risk of using such second-hand expression for diagnostic purposes seems to me to become overwhelming when the text being created is poetry. The whole procedure becomes vastly more insecure when we recognise that it cannot be simply assumed that the author's intention is to provide 'a sensitive and detailed account of the onset, course, and treatment of a mental disorder'.

This is the difficulty which I consider Kahn skates all too lightly around. He writes:

> For the purpose of this chapter, the Bible text will be considered as recording the words of a living person, and we shall look upon these words as being Job's own communications about his feelings and experiences.[4]

In my judgement this is a totally illegitimate procedure. Maimonides said the Book of Job was a fiction; I know of no competent biblical scholar who would disagree. Can we dismiss the reality of the text to say that 'for the purpose of this chapter' the Bible text will be considered to be something that it is not.[5]

---

4. Kahn, *Job's Illness*, 24.
5. I fear that at the base of Kahn's approach is a conviction not uncommon among those who have not had some experience of serious biblical scholarship. Put brutally, the conviction is that any event mentioned in the text happened, even if perhaps the record of it has suffered some distortion. The question is not seriously entertained as to whether the text intends the event as real, or intends to portray the 'how' of its happening. There are other pointers to this elsewhere in Kahn's book.

   For example, when he comes to the question of treatment, Kahn writes: 'In order to consider Job's illness in terms of therapy, we must bring in a dimension other than the one in which the story is told. The original framework is the cultural

These considerations so far concern what might be called the practical difficulties of using a text like the Book of Job for psychiatric diagnosis. There is a theoretical difficulty which is far more serious. If the purpose of the Book of Job is to explore the situation of the sufferer before God by deliberately setting up a limit case of the perfect human being whose suffering cannot be attributed to sin or human imperfection, then the entire endeavour is destroyed by the psychiatric analysis of Job as a flawed and obsessive personality.

This limit case of the totally innocent sufferer is precisely what I understand to be the central purpose of the Book of Job. The figure of Job is set up as one who is completely sinless. The book opens with the description of Job as 'blameless and upright, one who feared God and turned away from evil' (Job 1:1). This description is from the author. The taint of evil is kept so far from Job that he is portrayed even offering sacrifice for the possible sins of his children. Notice that this is the point seized on by Kahn to diagnose Job as obsessively scrupulous. But this is the precise opposite of the author's intention. The author has God repeat the description of Job as 'blameless and upright, one who fears God and turns away from evil' (1:8). Even Satan accepts the description, only impugning Job's motivation. For the author, Job is blameless. Chapter 31, the end of Job's speeches, is a massive re-emphasis of this point.

Job's blamelessness is critical to the whole enterprise of the book. The purpose of the book is to explore the situation of the sufferer before God. Job consistently affirms his innocence. His friends equally consistently and ever more scathingly deny it. In a key passage, Job affirms it against them:

> Far be it from me to say that you are right;
> till I die I will not put away my integrity from me.
> I hold fast my righteousness, and will not let it go;
> my heart does not reproach me for any of my days (27:5–6).

---

and religious one, and, ostensibly, it concerns a man who was tested by God in a wager with Satan, who survived the test (at least in the first place), and who later rebelled . . . We shall alter this framework by giving a naturalistic explanation of Job's experiences, and, for this purpose, we shall treat the religious framework as only part—although a very important part—of the influences which impinge upon the mind of an individual.' (Kahn, *Job's Illness*, 51). But we do not have access to Job's experiences or Job's mind, but only to the poetry of the author who situated that poetry within this religious framework.

While God is portrayed reproving Job—'Will you even put me in the wrong? Will you condemn me that you may be justified?' (40:8)— which is presumably the reference of Job's 'I despise myself and repent' (42:6), it is quite central to the book to realise that God is portrayed condemning the views of the friends as wrong, while maintaining Job as right.[6] God says to Eliphaz:

> My wrath is kindled against you and against your two friends; for you have not spoken of me what is right, as my servant Job has . . . I will accept his prayer not to deal with you according to your folly; for you have not spoken of me what is right, as my servant Job has (42:7–8).

The central message of the Book of Job is that the origin of human suffering is not to be found in the malice of God or in the fault of the human sufferer.

This is the point that Jack Kahn misses. For example, early in the piece, he writes:

> Possessions contribute to the image of the self, and when the possessions include family members, obsessional processes may be used in order to preserve their lives and control their fate. The obsessional activity provides a safeguard for the well-being of those who figure closely in the obsessional individual's life.
>
> Job's greatness and his perfection are thus connected with his possessions and the lives of his children. The breakdown of his physical and mental integration is associated with the loss of his children and his wealth. Far from being perfect, Job's personality contained features which in our own culture might be considered to be the precursor of mental breakdown.[7]

In Kahn's presentation, Job is the source of his own troubles. He has cracked under the pressure of his own obsessions. As a figure in literature, he is of no help to us in exploring the situation of innocent suffering before God. Instead Job becomes a paradigm of the patient in need of therapy.

---

6. Note that Job's 'I despise myself and repent' (42:6) cannot be understood as a retraction of the constant affirmations of his innocence. Any attempt to interpret it as such a retraction is negated by the emphatic condemnation of the three friends.
7. Kahn, *Job's Illness*, 15–16.

The message of the Book of Job

In brief, the message of the book of Job is: there is suffering which occurs in situations where neither God nor the human sufferer is responsible. Job is portrayed as attributing his suffering to God's hostility towards him and blaming God for it—and Job is portrayed as wrong. God's hostility, God's punishment, was not the source of Job's suffering.[8] The friends are portrayed as attributing Job's suffering to Job's sin—and they are portrayed as wrong. Job's sin was not the source of Job's suffering.

With these two blind alleys eliminated, in the context of the Book of Job there is only one possibility left. We can suffer without having brought it on ourselves by sin and without being estranged from God.

It would be a disaster if we lost the Book of Job as one of the greatest defences of human integrity before God, maintaining the right of the innocent sufferer to be innocent. I fear that Jack Kahn in transforming Job from perfect figure to obsessive perfectionist loses that defender of our integrity.

---

8. One could argue that the prologue presents God as testing Job, or at least permitting Satan to test him. But to attribute Job's suffering to divine testing would be to agree with the three friends (for example Job 5:17–18)—and the epilogue declares they are wrong. There is a tension between the prologue and the poetry. The prologue permits Job's suffering to result from God's pride, wounded by Satan's jibe. There is a sense in which this creates space to allow for the strength of the poetry's language against God. It is an unresolved tension between prologue and poetry, and it must remain unresolved. To resolve it in favour of the prologue would be to destroy the balance and purpose of the Book of Job.

Who Dares Wins: Reflections on the Story of David and Goliath and the Understanding of Human Freedom

This paper really begins where an article of mine in this year's *Australian Biblical Review* ended. The article discusses the story of David and Goliath in the books of Samuel, and in its last footnote refers to the two theological positions latent in interpretations of this story. In one understanding, God's role is to empower David to use his human talents and prowess in a courageous and daring act. But, in the more common interpretation, when the emphasis is shifted toward David as the little shepherd boy, God is no longer portrayed enabling full human potential to be realised, but instead is portrayed substituting divine wonder for human weakness.

Among the questions I wanted to ask was what do interpretations of such a story betray of our attitudes toward God and God's involvement in human existence? Why is it that the story of David and Goliath is so often told in a way that puts God in the role of parent rather than of partner? It occurred to me that it might not be hugely helpful to ask a conference on psychiatry and religion why God keeps getting cast in the parent role—there have been views on this among Freudians, which are not exactly what I want to explore. In this paper, my interest is to explore the story of David and Goliath as a model of divine-human interaction with God in the partner role, by which I mean God's role of empowering human beings to use their talents and prowess in courageous and full living rather than that of replacing human weakness with divine power. It is a feature that is strong in the stories of David as a whole, and it puts a healthy emphasis on human freedom in the relationship with God. For the story of David and Goliath, it could be summed up by using as a subtitle the SAS motto: Who dares wins!

There is no doubt that the story of David and Goliath, as it has come down to us in the present biblical text, is a highly complicated one. Equally though, there is no doubt that in the popular perception its interpretation is quite simple: it is a case of the little fellow against the massive warrior, of the underdog toppling the very definitely top dog, of weakness triumphing over power through divine grace. A recent scholarly commentary speaks of the story as follows:

> Of all David's exploits the one that is best known is the first. The story of the shepherd lad who by courage, cunning, and faith overcomes the gigantic champion of the enemy and brings victory to his people has all the elemental appeal of a fairy tale. The plot is uncomplicated and forceful, the characters almost archetypal . . . Here is David, small, apparently defenseless, with none of the bearing or equipment of a trained soldier . . . David has no real hope in force of arms, and despite his courage and wit he finally must rely on the one good hope that Judah, too, had in times of danger.[1]

Two things are really quite radically wrong with this, and yet they constantly escape notice. The first radical error is the conviction that David had no real hope in force of arms. In the passage quoted, Kyle McCarter rightly pays due tribute to David's courage, cunning, and wit. And it is true that the best equipment in the world is no use at all without the courage, cunning, and wit to operate it properly. But it is quite wrong to say that David had no real hope in force of arms: he had good standard military equipment, and in fact he had the most appropriate equipment for the occasion.

He had good standard military equipment. Slingstones are listed among the items in the ordinary military arsenal of the time. King Uzziah of Judah, for example, 'prepared for all the army shields, spears, helmets, coats of mail, bows, and stones for slinging' (2 Chron 26:14). When troops are assembled, slingers are reckoned among the specialist elite. In inter-tribal conflict, early in Israel's history, when the Benjaminites mustered their forces against the rest of Israel, it is noted that 'among all these were seven hundred picked men who were left-handed; every one could sling a stone at a hair, and not miss' (Judg 20:16). The sling is clearly singled out as a specialist weapon of remarkable accuracy.

---

1.   P Kyle McCarter, Jr, *I Samuel*, AB 8 (Garden City: Doubleday, 1980) 295 and 297.

He had the most appropriate equipment for the occasion. Goliath is portrayed as big and heavily armed; he is awesome enough to panic the whole army of Israel. As the story tells it, one may expect that on his own terms, with sword and spear, he is unbeatable. The best military manuals know, surely, that the only way to win in such a situation is not to meet the man on his own terms. The bigger his spear and the heavier his armour, the more likely he is to be a slow mover. The tactics needed to defeat him call for speed, surprise, and a long-range weapon. For David's purposes, the sling was the ideal weapon.

It is important to emphasise that the interpretation of a story comes from the text of the story, not from the historical detail we may be able to recover about it. The text does not make any comment on the aptness of the sling, neither to belittle it nor to approve of it. In the absence of contrary indications, it is legitimate to assume the ordinary expectations of the time: that the sling is to be understood as standard and appropriate equipment.

The second radical error in reading the David and Goliath story as a triumph of weakness over power through divine grace lies in the image of David as 'small and apparently defenseless'.[2] In the text of the story, this is quite definitely not the picture David paints of himself. David speaks of his own experience, when keeping his father's flocks. Faced by a lion or a bear, he went after it—so he is brave. He could catch up with it and force it to release its prey—so he is fast and tough. And if the beast turned on him, he could grab it under the jaw as a prelude to killing it—so he is not only tough, but his

---

2. This image has a very long history behind it. It is invited by the Septuagint, the ancient Greek translation, which refers to David in this story with a diminutive, *paidarion*, little boy. In fact, *paidarion* is the most common translation for the Hebrew word *na'ar*, very often rendered 'youth', but having a wide gamut of meanings (see note 6, below). But unless one were very familiar with the text of Samuel, the use of the diminutive would be an invitation to picture David as the little shepherd boy. Josephus, the first-century Jewish historian, in his paraphrase of the biblical text, has: 'Saul admired the lad's daring and courage, but could not place full confidence in him by reason of his years, because of which, he said, he was too feeble to fight with a skilled warrior' (*Jewish Antiquities*, VI, 181). This is remarkable, when we consider that a little earlier Josephus, rendering 1 Sam 16:18, referred to David as 'an excellent soldier' (*Jewish Antiquities* 167).

reflexes are very good (1 Sam 17:34–35).[3] A little reflection on this autobiographical passage shows why David was, in fact, the ideal person to take up the Philistine's challenge. Instead of man–to–man combat with the huge warrior, skilled in the use of his own weapons, David will use the tactics of the unexpected. Speed and surprise may get him within slingshot range before the Philistine realises his danger and takes cover behind his shield; the quality of his reflexes will ensure that his slingstone does not miss. His demonstrated courage and toughness will enable him to carry it off. This is not a small and apparently defenceless little shepherd boy. He may be the youngest of his father's sons, but that does not say anything about his size or age. If he were meant to be thought of as small, would the storyteller have made so incongruous a move as to have Saul, who towered head and shoulders over Israel, offer David his armour?

So, even on the evidence of the text as we have it now, the archetypal image of the underdog facing hopeless odds is quite misleading. David is the right man for the job, and he has the right weapon for the job.

When the history of the text is explored further, this understanding becomes even more evident. As we noted at the beginning, the text of this story is highly complicated; there are strong grounds for arguing against its unity. This is not the place to go through the exegetical examination of the text in detail.[4] We may just indicate the

---

3. A recent article by a young German scholar simply asserts that a redactor attempted to lessen the tension between David as man of war and the child as peaceful shepherd by inserting 17:33–35 (Theodor Seidl, 'David statt Saul: Göttliche Legitimation und menschliche Kompetenz des Königs als Motive der Redaktion von I Sam 16–18', in *ZAW* 98 [1986]: 39–55, see 42). No evidence is adduced to support the suggestion, and in fact there is none available. It appears to be another example of the conviction that the youngest son and shepherd has to be 'small and apparently defenseless'.

4. I have gone into these issues in more detail in the *Australian Biblical Review* article referred to ('From Philistine to Throne', in *AusBR* 34 [1986]), some of which is repeated here. Briefly, the difficulties are:

   1) 1 Sam 17:12 gives the impression of being the beginning of a new story.

   2) 17:15 gives the impression of being a harmonising addition, holding together differing traditions of David at Saul's camp and David back at the family farm.

   3) 17:16 is inconsistent with its context which implies surprise and consternation at the appearance of the Philistine champion (17:24–25).

   4) 17:19 repeats details about the locality already supplied in 17:2.

main points. David is introduced in the middle of the story (v 12) rather as though it were the beginning; the confrontation with the Philistines and the appearance of Goliath on the scene is repeated rather as though it had not been told before (vv 19–24); one verse has Goliath killed by the slingstone (v 50), while in the next verse David takes Goliath's own sword and kills him with it; finally, after Saul has sent David out with his blessing (v 37), he is portrayed as surprised to see him and knowing nothing about him (vv 55–58).

To jump from evidence to conclusions, without passing through a full discussion of the arguments, here, as often in biblical narratives, we have two stories combined into one. What is most unusual, however, is that the text of one of the two stories is preserved intact in the Greek translation of the Bible, the Septuagint.[5] When the stories are separated, all the difficulties about unity disappear.

In the version which has been preserved intact in the Greek, which omits vv 12–31, David is standing at Saul's side, as his armour-bearer (cf, 1 Sam 16:14–23). When Saul and all Israel are portrayed as 'dismayed and greatly afraid' (17:11), David is right there beside

---

5) 17:23 repeats a full identification of the Philistine champion, already supplied in 17:4.

6) the mass flight and fear suggests that this is intended as the first appearance of the Philistine (see also v 20b), despite the harmonisation in v 23, 'he spoke the same words as before'.

7) 17:50 has the Philistine killed by the sling-stone, while in v 51 David takes the Philistine's sword, kills him with it, and cuts off his head.

8) 17:55 gives no indication of Saul's already having had a conversation with David (cf vv 32–39)—it is not merely a question of not knowing his name.

9) 17:57b is in conflict with 17:54a, at least in the narrative sequence;

10) 18:5 is a conclusion, with a perspective extending beyond the events of the day; 18:6, on the other hand, relates immediately to the combat with the Philistine.

11) 18:10–11 is a doublet of 19:9–10 and appears better placed in the context of chapter 19.

5. More accurately, in one manuscript tradition of the Septuagint. The story which is preserved intact in the Greek (while combined with the other in the Hebrew) is contained in 1 Sam 17:1–11, 32–40, 42–48a, 49, 51–54; 18:6a*–9, 12a, 13. The other story, not represented in this Greek manuscript tradition, is contained in 1 Samuel 17:12–31, 41, 48b, 50, 55–18:6a*, 18:10–11, 12b, 17–19, 21b, 29b–30. For further details, see 'From Philistine to Throne'. This latter story tends toward the folktale form of the young man who, by deeds of derring-do, wins the hand of a princess in marriage and half of her father's kingdom.

him—in the story and in the text, since vv 12–31 are omitted—to say,
'Let no man's heart fail because of him; your servant will go and fight
with this Philistine' (v 32). The story unfolds as a contrast between
Saul and David. This is a crucial moment for Israel; it is also a crucial moment in the story, and a turning point in the lives of Saul and
David. Here they are presented side by side, Saul dismayed by un-
kingly fear and David bearing himself in thoroughly kingly fashion.
It is the king's role to be military leader and deliverer of his people,
but Saul is depicted as unmanned by fear; the deliverer role passes to
David. The story continues the contrast. Saul is portrayed as making his judgement on grounds of military appearances (there is no
discussion of the sling here), and David is portrayed trusting in God.
Even the brief exchange over the armour points in this direction.
Goliath bases his confidence on the same grounds as Saul—hardly
flattering to the latter.

The primary contrast in this version of the story is between Saul,
dismayed, afraid, and unmanned, and David, spirited, courageous,
and confident. Saul had been anointed king to deliver Israel. Bereft
of God's spirit (16:14), he is unable to deliver his people; instead,
he quivers in fear. It is David who will demonstrate his leadership
qualities, who will deliver Israel from this Philistine threat, and who
will show that God is with him. The victory over the Philistine is the
beginning of David's move toward the throne over Israel. The storyteller saw it that way and told the story in order that we would see it
the same way.

We should not be led astray by the dialogue with Saul. Saul says,
'You are not able to go against this Philistine to fight with him; for
you are but a youth, and he has been a man of war from his youth' (v
33). The meaning should be quite clear: you are but a beginner, while
he is a very experienced campaigner.[6] Interestingly, Saul does not ask

---

6. The language needs comment. In 17:33, the contrast is not between the boy and
   the man, but between the inexperienced soldier (youth) and the experienced
   challenger who has been a warrior from his youth. The Hebrew word for 'youth'
   here has its frequent sense of young soldier, capable of killing (2 Sam 2:12–16)
   and of intercourse (1 Sam 21:5). H-P Stähli, in his monograph on the term
   (*Knabe-Jüngling-Knecht* [BET 7; Frankfurt a. M: Peter Lang, 1978]), shows the
   range of its meanings from newborn child (1 Sam 1:22) to royal overseer (1 Kgs
   11:28), as well as the two basic senses underlying these; the precise nuance is
   determined by the context. Here, in 1 Sam 17:33, in my judgement quite wrongly,

David how he proposes to defeat the Philistine. For the storyteller, at one level, Saul is to be seen as a dismayed, despairing man; and, at another level altogether, it would spoil the story to unveil the ending too soon.

There is also the potential trap that in order to depict the despairing king in contrast to his spirited successor, the storyteller has to have Saul insisting that David's situation is hopeless and that he has no chance. Why do we walk into that trap by assuming that Saul's judgement is motivated by the physical stature of puny David instead of by the dispirited despair of a king abandoned by God's spirit? David's description of himself should have made the matter clear.[7]

My suspicion is that people interpret the David and Goliath story in the usual way because people like to envisage God in that way; that there is a tendency in many people to look to God to do the impossible, to expect God to slay all their Goliaths for them. Which leads to my theological concern: which is the more helpful way to envisage divine-human relations? Is it more helpful to conceive of God supporting us by filling in the gaps left by human weakness? Or is it more helpful to see God empowering us in the use of our talents and strengths?

I find it useful to reflect on the two images presented by the differing interpretations of the David and Goliath story. If David is seen as the defenceless little shepherd boy, then what reveals—to all those assembled and to us—that God saves not with sword or spear but will give Goliath into David's hand (v 47) is the fact that such an unlikely weapon as a slingstone finds its way from the shepherd's sling into the Philistine's forehead. On the other hand, if David is seen as tough and strong, with excellent reflexes, and equipped with a dangerously accurate weapon, then the evidence of God's saving power is that this

---

Stähli gives it the sense of 'half-grown youth', without a full discussion (*Knabe-Jüngling-Knecht*, 91–92), rejecting HJ Stoebe's juxtaposition of 1 Sam 16:14–23 with 17:1–11, 32–54 ('Goliathperikope', 405–10, *Das erste Buch Samuelis*, 335) which is assumed here.

7. Another misleading factor comes from the combination with the other story. There David is explicitly portrayed as a shepherd, who goes directly from the family farm to the military camp (vv 12–30). It is probably the influence of this picture which accounts for the occurrence, in 17:40, of the usual words for shepherd's bag as a gloss for the very unusual term translated pouch or wallet. It is unlikely that it was the other way round.

man had the courage to risk facing a fearsome foe when everyone else was desperate with fear.[8]

The 'thoroughgoing worldliness' of the Succession Narrative, or Story of David's Later Years (2 Samuel 9–20; 1 Kings1–2), has long been noted. There is a similarly secular streak in the stories of David's rise to power in Israel which follow his career from his victory over Goliath to his accession to the throne over all Israel. This is all the more remarkable when we consider that these stories were told with the evident intention of saying that David got to the throne of Israel because God was with him—yet God is never given a principal role in the action.[9] Direct divine intervention is basically restricted to the anointings by Samuel, and these are a century or so later than the original stories.[10] So, the interpretation of the story of David and Goliath given here can be seen as paradigmatic for the other Davidic stories.

---

8. Heavily embellished by novellistic imagination, this is the version portrayed in irreverent detail by Joseph Heller, in chapter 3 of *God Knows* (New York: Alfred A Knopf, 1984).

9. There are only three explicit references to God by the narrator: 2 Sam 11:27; 12:24; 17:14; see Gerhard von Rad, *Old Testament Theology* (2 volumes; Edinburgh: Oliver and Boyd, 1962–65) 1.312–17.

10. For example: according to the text, it is David's quick reflexes which save him from Saul's spear-cast, not God's intervening hand (1 Sam 19:9–10). It is Michal's intuition and not God's revelation which warns David to save his life by climbing out the window and escaping into the night (19:11–17). It is David and Jonathan's careful checking out of Saul's intentions which later saves David's skin, not any information from the Almighty (20:1–42). Even in a fascinating case where there is the explicit use of divination to inquire of God, in the anecdote about the Philistine siege of Keilah, while God is reported saying, 'Go, do it!', the battle is reported as David's, not God's. Subsequently, when divination reveals that the townsfolk of Keilah are going to betray their deliverer to Saul, there is no question of divine wrath or divine protection—David and his men simply melt into the mountains (23:1–14). The killing which clears the way for David is done by purely human means: the Philistines kill Saul and his sons (31:1–7); a vengeance-seeking brother kills Saul's general (2 Sam 2:18–23; 3:22–30); a couple of disloyal mercenaries kill Saul's successor (4:5–12). In all this, God is not explicitly involved at all. And yet the narrator's judgement on all these stories was, 'And David had success in all his undertakings, for the LORD was with him' (1 Sam 18:14).

    See my *Of Prophets and Kings: A Late Ninth-Century Document* (1 Samuel 1–2 Kings 10) (CBQMS 17; Washington: Catholic Biblical Association of America, 1986).

In my judgement, the story of David and Goliath is also a helpful model for talking about divine action and human freedom. It is far easier to tell a story than to spell out such matters in cold discourse. What I believe is important to us, in this present context, is conviction about general attitudes. The systematic treatment, which hammers out details of expression and explores all the implications and ramifications, is for professional theologians to elaborate. The task of reconciling God's attributes and human freedom is notoriously difficult. At this conference last year, I admitted to a preference for preserving, as far as possible, the intelligibility of human freedom and reserving mystery to the sphere of the divine, where it most appropriately belongs.

In the interpretation of the David and Goliath story in which David is the small and defenceless little shepherd, God is in an obviously parent-type role. It is a theology which I find uncongenial and unsatisfactory. It generates expectations of God which are demeaning for the creature and unfair for the Creator. It frequently leaves the image of God in considerable need of redemption. I have strong preference for the sort of theology which is able to recognise that David was the right person with the right equipment for the task. In this model of God as partner, what God did for David was to enable David to do what he could do for himself. In the metaphor of the David and Goliath story, David got his start in public life not through the equivalent of a divine thunderbolt but through a well-aimed sling-stone and the strength of his own nerve.

To put a little flesh on God's activity as enabling human beings in their living, I would point to three areas of significance to life. One is that of basic trust. I would hope for a theology that could speak of a God who is worthy of our trust. Another is that of fundamental love. I would hope for a theology that could speak of a God who is capable of unconditional love for us. Thirdly, there is the question of the articulation of ideals. I would hope for a theology that could present a God whose being and love challenges us to the highest ideals of human living. The combination of basic trust and unconditional love with the challenge of high ideals is surely enabling and empowering for rich human living.

As counterpoint to these reflections on two images of God, there are two versions of a saying, popularly attributed to St. Ignatius Loyola, the founder of the Jesuits. The usual version of the saying runs: pray as if everything depended on God and work as if every-thing depended on you. In the formality of prayer, at least, God is portrayed as the doer on whom all depends. The other version, found in Jesuit documents, is exactly the opposite: pray as if everything depended on you and work as if everything depended on God.[11] In such a spirituality, God is a companion and a partner, but not a sub-stitute or a replacement.

---

11. The Latin reads: *Haec prima sit agendorum regula: sic Deo fide, quasi rerum successus omnis a te, nihil a Deo penderet: ita tamen iis operam omnem admove, quasi tu nihil, Deus omnia solus sit facturus* (Thesaurus Spiritualis Societatis Jesu, 1948, 480). More adequately translated: 'Let this be the first rule of action—so trust in God as if success depended entirely on you, and not on God at all; but so give yourself to the task as if you were doing nothing and God alone were to do it all.' Regrettably, I am told that the attribution of either version to Ignatius remains unsubstantiated; I suspect the one given here would have received his preference.

Which leads to my theological concern: it is far easier to tell a story than to spell out theological matters in cold discourse.

CPSIA information can be obtained
at www.ICGtesting.com
Printed in the USA
JSHW011129030520
5466JS00001B/64